The Tough Kid®

Tool Box

WILLIAM R. JENSON, PH.D.

GINGER RHODE, PH.D.

H. KENTON REAVIS, ED.D.

Published in the United States by
Pacific Northwest Publishing
2451 Willamette St.
Eugene, Oregon 97405

ISBN 978-1-59909-034-4

Originally published as *The Tough Kid Tool Box*.
Original ISBN: 978-1-57035-124-2. Publisher: Sopris West.

Pacific
Northwest
Publishing

Eugene, Oregon | www.pacificnwpublish.com

Table of Contents

Section 4 • Behavioral Contracting (continued)

Section 5 • Tracking Procedures 65

Section 6 • Unique Reinforcers 75

Section 6 • Unique Reinforcers (continued)

Section 7 • General Interventions 111

About the Authors

William R. Jenson, Ph.D.

Dr. William R. Jenson is a professor and past chair of the Department of Educational Psychology at the University of Utah. He received his Ph.D. in School Psychology/Applied Behavior Analysis from Utah State University in 1975. He directed the Adolescent Residential Unit in Las Vegas, Nevada, and the Children's Behavior Therapy Unit (CBTU) for Salt Lake Mental Health. CBTU is a day hospital program for severely emotionally disturbed and autistic children. Dr. Jenson's interests include behavior management for severe behavior problems, behavioral assessment, school-based interventions, parent training, applied technology, and meta-analytic research. He has authored and coauthored more than one hundred articles, chapters, and books, including *The Tough Kid Book, Tough Kid Tool Box, Tough Kid Parent Book, Tough Kid New Teacher Book, Tough Kid Principal's Briefcase, Understanding Childhood Behavior Disorders, Structured Teaching, Best Practices: Behavioral and Educational Strategies, Teaching Behaviorally Disordered Students: Preferred Practices, School-Based Interventions for Students with Behavior Problems, Functional Assessment and Intervention Program, Get'm on Task* computer program, and several others.

Ginger Rhode, Ph.D.

Dr. Rhode is the Deputy Superintendent for Academic Achievement in the Canyons School District in Sandy, Utah. Previous assignments in other school districts have included Director of Special Education, Director of Federal and State Programs, elementary school principal, junior high school vice principal, and teacher in elementary and secondary classrooms for severe behavior disordered/emotionally disturbed students. Dr. Rhode is an adjunct faculty member at the University of Utah in the Educational Psychology Department. She has taught numerous university classes and has published many books, journal articles, book chapters, and professional papers. Her main areas of interest and expertise include classroom and schoolwide management, social skills training, generalization and maintenance of behavior, legal issues affecting students with disabilities, and providing a rigorous academic environment for all students.

H. Kenton Reavis, Ed.D.

Dr. Ken Reavis, our honored colleague, was Coordinator of the Comprehensive System of Personnel Development and Specialist for Behavior Disorders and Discipline in the Services for the At Risk Section of the Utah State Office of Education. His extensive educational experience in the field as classroom teacher, university professor, and administrator was reflected in his research, writing, and presentations. Dr. Reavis's career focused on student management, discipline, school climate, noncompliance, school assistance teams, and prereferral strategies. His work continues to benefit teachers, administrators, resource personnel, and parents. Dr. Reavis passed away in 2001.

Introduction

The *Tough Kid Tool Box* serves to both complement and supplement the first and second editions of *The Tough Kid Book*. The *Tough Kid Tool Box* parallels *The Tough Kid Book*, but gives additional in-depth explanations and techniques that you can use in everyday situations. It is most efficient to first read *The Tough Kid Book* and then refer to *The Tough Kid Tool Box*'s major sections. However, it is not absolutely necessary to read *The Tough Kid Book* before finding this book useful, because each of the tools provided is accompanied by step-by-step instructions.

This book contains sections on unique procedures such as the Yes/No Program, Mystery Motivators, Home Notes, self-monitoring, contracting, and others. There is also a general section that includes an activity schedule for the classroom, peer tutoring forms, Advertising for Success forms, and others.

Each of the seven sections of *The Tough Kid Tool Box* provides explanations of the interventions included. Each section of the book begins with a definition of the intervention, a specific description of the intervention, and complete steps for implementing the technique. In addition, there are many troubleshooting suggestions that offer practical solutions to problems that might arise. "Making it even better" suggestions offer several variations on the interventions that will make them even more effective or unique.

Possibly the best feature of *The Tough Kid Tool Box*, however, is the number of practical forms, or tools, that you can copy and use. These tools are very helpful in saving teacher time. Forms such as the Home Note, Mystery Motivator, and self-monitoring forms have been used and debugged with many actual Tough Kids.

The tools appear at the end of each section. You can copy the forms directly from the book. The CD contains electronic versions of each form in English and in Spanish (see the examples on the next page). Where appropriate, these forms are set up so you can fill them out on your computer using Adobe Reader before printing them. See the "Using the CD" file on the CD for more information on how to use Adobe Reader to fill out forms.

If you bought the book for your classroom, feel free to copy the tools and use them with your students. However, you are given permission to use them only with your students in your classroom. If another teacher wants to use the tools, then please have that teacher buy his or her own book. This is similar to buying software that is licensed for use with only one computer. Each book and CD should be used for only one classroom or by one professional in his or her work.

Good luck with *The Tough Kid Tool Box*. Remember, the interventions have been designed to make education fun and positive for Tough Kids. If education is positive and well planned, Tough Kids turn out to be great kids!

Mystery Motivators

def•i•ni•tion

Mystery Motivators are incentive systems designed to deliver random rewards for appropriate behavior. They can be used with single students, teams, or a whole class. Their use depends on you and the behaviors you want to increase (e.g., academic assignments completed, promptness, good lunchroom behavior, few classroom rules broken, etc.) or decrease (e.g., noncompliance, fighting, swearing, talk-outs, or academic errors).

de•scrip•tion

The Mystery Motivator tools (Reproducibles 1-1 through 1-9) provided in this section are all basically the same form with different pictures added to appeal to individual students. The squares are labeled with the days of the week, with a bonus square at the end of the week. An invisible-ink pen is used to indicate which days are reward days by putting an "M" in the square(s) of reward days. A developer pen is required for the student or students (if this intervention is being used with teams or with the whole class) to color the square to see if an "M" appears. If an "M" appears, a reward is given for that day if the pre-specified criterion has been met. Each Mystery Motivator also includes a Comments Section that can be used to give positive feedback to your students.

Steps for Implementing Mystery Motivators

STEP 1 Select some basic rewards for students to earn with the Mystery Motivator. This can be accomplished by watching what they do frequently (this is what rewards them), keeping track of what they ask you for (this is also a hint about what rewards them), asking them for suggestions for rewards, using a menu or checklist, or looking at Chapter 2 of *The Tough Kid Book* for ideas. Make a list of at least ten rewards that do not take a lot of time or cost a lot of money. It helps to think like a kid in coming up with this list.

STEP 2 Write one selected reward on a piece of paper, put it in a sealed envelope, and do not tell the students what it is. If you are working with only one student, the envelope may be stapled or taped to the Mystery Motivator form and kept at your desk. If the Mystery Motivator is being used with the whole class, the envelope may be stapled or taped to the Mystery Motivator form and hung at the front of the room.

"It helps to think like a kid."

TECHNIQUE TIP

Draw question marks on the Mystery Motivator envelope, refer to it often, point to it during the day, and give the students hints about what is inside (e.g., "It is brown and awesome."). However, the students should not be told what the reward is. ~

STEP 3 Define the behavior you want students to increase or decrease. This definition should be objective and specific. If the behavior cannot be seen or measured, it is probably a bad choice. (Improve your attitude, be more responsible, be a good citizen, and do better work are all poor choices because they are too general.) Some good specific choices include be in your seat ready to work before the bell, finish your assignment with at least 70% accuracy, follow classroom rules, hand in completed homework on time, and receive good or excellent reports from the bus driver. A whole class might need to have more positive marks on the What If? Chart than rule-breaking checkmarks (see Section 7 of this book).

TECHNIQUE TIP

It helps to write the exact behavior and the criteria you have selected on the Mystery Motivator sheet for the students to see. ~

STEP 4 Purchase a set of invisible- and developer-ink pens at

www.crayola.com. The invisible-ink pen is used to write an "M" in the squares for reward days. After the ink dries, students should not be able to tell on which squares an "M" has been written. Days for no reward are left blank.

TECHNIQUE TIP

Invisible/developer-ink pens can be purchased at www.crayola.com. Alternately, you can use a regular pen and cover the numbers with stickers that can be removed. ~

STEP 5 If the students meet the pre-specified criteria, they get to color in the square for that day with the developer pen. If an "M" appears after the coloring, the envelope is opened and the specified reward is given immediately.

TECHNIQUE TIP

If you are working with a group of students or the whole class, the student who worked the hardest that day may be asked to color in the square to see if the reward will be given. ~

STEP 6 If no "M" appears after the student colors the square with the developer pen, congratulate the participating students on their behavior (describe how well they have performed) and tell the students that tomorrow could be a reward day.

STEP 7 An important factor is the number of reward "M"s that are placed in the squares. In the beginning, you should provide at least two or three per week until the students become adept at the behavior. Then the squares can be thinned out to one or two per week. It is also important to place the reward squares back-to-back occasionally. For example, if an "M" is placed in the Monday square, then sometimes one should also be placed in the Tuesday square. If this is not done, the students quickly learn that if they are rewarded one day, then the next day they will not be rewarded. If so, they generally stop trying on the day after the reward.

STEP 8 The bonus square on the Mystery Motivator form may also be used as an additional incentive for the students. A number up to five may be written with the invisible-ink pen in the bonus square at the beginning of the week. At the end of the week, the students get to color in the bonus square with the developer pen to reveal the invisible number. If the students meet the criteria for the target behavior the number of times specified in the bonus square (or higher) that week, a bonus reward is given. The bonus reward may either be known to the students ahead of time or a surprise.

STEP 9 Comments are important, particularly if you are using the Mystery Motivator with a single student and you encourage the student to take the Mystery Motivator sheet home. Make the comments positive. Avoid such comments as "Jeffery has done well but could do even better" or "Marla is trying but has so much more potential." These are actually punishing comments. Make the comments purely positive: "Jeffery got a 75% on his spelling test—what a great job!" or "What a star! Marla handed in her homework each day this week."

TECHNIQUE TIP

If you are using the Mystery Motivator with a single student, ask the student to take the Mystery Motivator form home and tape it to the refrigerator. The student will like the idea because of the picture, and his or her parents will appreciate your positive comments. ~

Troubleshooting Mystery Motivators

.... *Scenario 1* ....

PROBLEM: Sometimes students stop working when they receive a reward. The next day they assume they will not get a Mystery Motivator reward.

SOLUTION: Randomly place rewards back-to-back. If the students are rewarded one day, have a reward programmed for the very next day.

.... *Scenario 2* ....

PROBLEM: A student complains about the Mystery Motivator reward and wants a different one.

SOLUTION: A rule should be established that if the students complain or want a different reward, they lose that reward for the day.

.... *Scenario 3* ....

PROBLEM: A student indicates that she does not want to participate in the Mystery Motivator program. She is not interested.

SOLUTION: Indicate that nonparticipation is OK, but the student will lose a valued privilege such as recess or break time when the behavior selected for change is not exhibited. For example, the student says the program is "stupid" and she is not going to do the assigned seatwork. Simply withdraw a valued privilege when the student does not work. Indicate that when she is ready to participate, she can get the privilege back and work for a Mystery Motivator.

.... *Scenario 4* ....

PROBLEM: A student tries to cheat by holding up the Mystery Motivator envelope and trying to read what type of reward is written on the piece of paper.

SOLUTION: Write the reward in light pencil and fold over the paper. Or if you observe the student trying to read the reward paper in the envelope, suspend the program for one day for cheating.

.... *Scenario 5* ....

PROBLEM: A student coloring in that day's square tries to partially color in the next day's box by "accidentally" getting ink into the box. This is done to see if part of an "M" appears.

SOLUTION: Make the invisible-ink "M" very small in the box. Or suspend the program for one day because the student tried to cheat.

Making Mystery Motivators Even Better

1 Possibly one of the best ways to make a Mystery Motivator even better is to use it with groups of students in teams. For example, assign each student to a team of three students. If all three students turn in their homework first thing in the morning (or accomplish the specified behavior), then the team colors in a square on their team form to see if an "M" appears, indicating that all of them get the reward. If some of the students do not turn in their homework (or accomplish the specified behavior), their team does not get to color in a square.

2 Use the Mystery Motivator with the whole class to improve a behavior. For

example, if no one is tardy on any one morning, the Mystery Motivator square is colored in to see if the whole class gets a reward (e.g., 15 minutes free time, a popcorn party, a story).

> **TECHNIQUE TIP**
>
> If one student chronically fails or sets the other members up to lose, make that student a one-member team. ~

3 Give hints or make a game out of trying to guess what is in the Mystery Motivator envelope. This can be done at the beginning of the day to enhance motivation and increase anticipation. Write the students' guesses on the board to see who came the closest.

4 Use the Mystery Motivator with a special secret number for a particular behavior. Put the Mystery Motivator in the middle of the blackboard with the number written on the back of it. The students will not be told the number. For example, the number might be the limit of classroom rules that can be broken that day. At the end of the day, take the envelope down and read the mystery number. If the number of rule violations is below that mystery number, the whole class gets the Mystery Motivator reward. If the number of broken rules is higher than the mystery number, the class does not receive the reward. If the secret number is used as a criterion, it is important to vary it each day.

5 Combine the Mystery Motivator with other techniques featured in this book and *The Tough Kid Book.* Good techniques to combine with the Mystery Motivator are reward Spinners, Home Notes, contracts, the "Sure I Will" Program, and Classroom Behavior Bingo.

Mystery Motivators Reproducible Tools

Both Spanish and English versions of all
REPRODUCIBLE TOOLS
appear on the CD.

MYSTERY MOTIVATOR

MON	TUE	WED	THUR	FRI	BONUS

Name: _____

Comments: _____

_____

_____

_____

Tank Up for a
MYSTERY MOTIVATOR

MON	TUE	WED	THUR	FRI	BONUS

Name: _____

Comments: _____

_____

_____

_____

Rock and Roll for a
MYSTERY MOTIVATOR

MON	TUE	WED	THUR	FRI	BONUS

Name: _____

Comments: _____

_____

_____

See pp. 3–6 for suggestions for use.

Tough Kid Tool Box

FOR GRADES

K-6

Work Like a Dog for a

MYSTERY MOTIVATOR

MON	TUE	WED	THUR	FRI	BONUS

Name: _____

Comments: _____

_____

_____

_____

See pp. 3-6 for suggestions for use.

Tough Kid Tool Box

K-6 FOR GRADES

Whirl In for a
MYSTERY MOTIVATOR

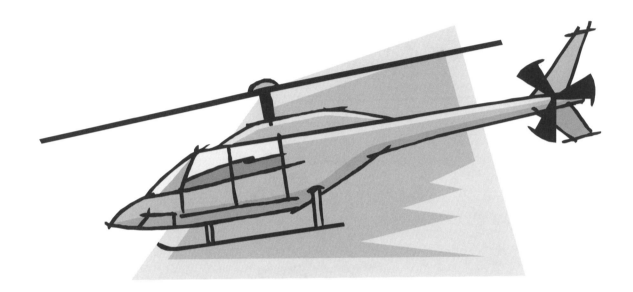

MON	TUE	WED	THUR	FRI	BONUS

Name: _____

Comments: _____

_____

_____

_____

Tough Kid Tool Box   K-6   FOR GRADES

Graduate to a
MYSTERY MOTIVATOR

MON	TUE	WED	THUR	FRI	BONUS

Name: _____

Comments: _____

_____

_____

_____

Drive Away With a
MYSTERY MOTIVATOR

MON	TUE	WED	THUR	FRI	BONUS

_____

_____

_____

_____

_____

Tough Kid Tool Box   K-6   FOR GRADES

Be Cool for a
MYSTERY MOTIVATOR

MON	TUE	WED	THUR	FRI	BONUS

Name: _____

Comments: _____

_____

_____

_____

See pp. 3-6 for suggestions for use.

REPRODUCIBLE 1-9

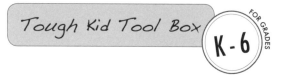

Tough Kid Tool Box

FOR GRADES

K-6

Don't Crash Without a
MYSTERY MOTIVATOR

MON	TUE	WED	THUR	FRI	BONUS

Name: _____

Comments: _____

_____

_____

_____

The Home Note Program

def•i•ni•tion

A Home Note (or Home-to-School Note) is an informational note that goes from the classroom to home and back to school. It exchanges information between the family and teacher about a student's classroom behavior and/or academic performance.

de•scrip•tion

The Home Note is generally filled out by the teacher with global ratings for specific behavior and/or academic progress. The note is then signed or initialed by the teacher and sent home. The note is reviewed by the student's family, signed or initialed by one of them, and then sent back to the teacher. Good Home Note programs also have the parent apply some type of rewards for good classroom performance and behavior and mild reductive consequences for poor performance and behavior. There are two types of basic notes: a daily Home Note and a weekly Home Note.

Steps for Implementing a Home Note Program

 **STEP 1** Decide what type of Home Note is necessary. Daily Home Notes are helpful when the program is first started because they keep parents informed and allow daily consequences for behavior. Weekly notes are helpful when the student is performing well or the parents need to be informed less frequently. Both types of forms (Reproducibles 2-2 and 2-3) are provided in this section.

STEP 2 Set up a conference with the student's parent(s). Solicit their cooperation, ask them their goals, and help them decide on the rewards and reductive consequences at home for the behavior and/or performance on the note.

TECHNIQUE TIP

Good positive reinforcement in the home for elementary students includes extra television time, an extended bedtime, or a chance at a Mystery Motivator reward (see Section 1 of this book and Chapter 2 of *The Tough Kid Book*.) **Reductive consequences** for elementary students can include earlier bedtimes, grounding on the weekend, temporary loss of a favorite toy, no television, or loss of part of an allowance. ~

"A Home Note exchanges information between the parents and teacher."

TECHNIQUE TIP

Good classroom behaviors to target include being on task, immediately doing what the teacher asks, being prepared, and following the classroom rules. Good academic behaviors to target include ratings in the basic subjects of reading, math, and spelling; completing assignments neatly; and handing in homework on time. ~

TECHNIQUE TIP

To help choose appropriate behaviors to include on the Home Note, see the "Importance of Classroom Behaviors (Teacher Rating Form)" at the end of this section or its corresponding picture icons (see Reproducible 2-1) included in this section's reproducible tools. ~

TECHNIQUE TIP

Positive reinforcement for secondary students can include access to driving, use of the telephone, music, extended curfews, etc.

Reductive consequences may include loss of part of an allowance, loss of phone privileges, missing a desired activity, or completing extra chores at home. ~

STEP 3 In the conference with the family, decide on the behaviors that should be included on the Home Note. It is best to mix classroom behavior and academic behavior. No more than five behaviors for elementary students or ratings from seven class periods for secondary students should be included.

STEP 4 In the conference with the family, decide on how the behaviors should be rated. Some Home Notes provided in the reproducible tools for this section have built-in rating scales. The ratings should be simple and global.

TECHNIQUE TIP

Faces (smiley, neutral, or frowny) and plus signs/zero signs are good for rating the target behaviors of elementary students. For secondary students, a numerical rating (from 1 to 3—unsatisfactory, average, and great) may be used. Another option is listing the ratings (e.g., great, average, unsatisfactory) and circling the rating in ink. ~

> ⚠ **CAUTION**
>
> A minus sign is a poor rating symbol because it can be changed into a plus sign too easily by the student.

STEP 5 In the conference with the family, decide what type of reductive consequences and positive reinforcement should correspond to each rating. Remember, the note should be mostly positive, not negative.

TECHNIQUE TIP

For elementary students, it is suggested that for each smiley face earned, a student receives 10 minutes of extra television time or has bedtime delayed for 10 minutes (5 smileys = 50 minutes extra). For each frowny face, television time is reduced by 10 minutes or the bedtime is moved up 10 minutes (3 frowny faces = to bed 30 minutes early).

For secondary students, the ratings can be designed for time driving the family car, gallons of gas provided for their use, time to use the telephone, or listening to music on the family sound system. ~

STEP 6 In the conference with the family, suggest that no excuse from the student be accepted for not taking the note home or returning it to school. Common student excuses include:

- "I forgot."
- "There was a substitute teacher."
- "There were special activities at school, and I didn't go to class."

TECHNIQUE TIP

For elementary students, a good reductive consequence for not taking the note home is going to bed one hour early with loss of television privileges. For not returning the note to school, loss of recess or free time privileges plus a call home to the family is appropriate.

For secondary students, a good reductive consequence for not taking the note home is loss of driving or telephone privileges. If the note continues to not be taken, grounding can be used (e.g., one day for each day the note is not taken home). ~

STEP 7 Explain the procedure to the student after meeting with the family. Indicate: (1) how the Home Note will be rated and used, (2) the positive reinforcement and mildly reductive consequences that will be included, and (3) that no excuses will be accepted for not taking the note home or returning it to school.

TECHNIQUE TIP

Outline for the student the steps that should be followed to get the note rated if there is a substitute teacher (e.g., an office secretary or counselor could help the student) or for special situations such as assembly or movie (e.g., come to the teacher before class or ask for a rating during the assembly). ~

STEP 8 Begin the Home Note program on a Monday. Rate the student's performance, and if possible, try to give the student positive ratings for the first several days. After the note has been rated, initial the note and give it to the student. Remind the student that no excuses will be accepted for loss of the note.

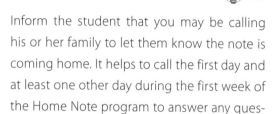

TECHNIQUE TIP

Inform the student that you may be calling his or her family to let them know the note is coming home. It helps to call the first day and at least one other day during the first week of the Home Note program to answer any questions and encourage the family to carry out their part of the program. ~

Troubleshooting Home Notes

·············· *Scenario 1* ··············

PROBLEM: The student loses the Home Note.

SOLUTION: Have the student lose an important privilege either at home or at school. For example, the student could lose his television privileges and go to bed an hour early. Or the student could lose a school privilege such as all recess time for the day. Remember, do not accept excuses for a lost note.

·············· *Scenario 2* ··············

PROBLEM: The student forges or changes a signature on the note or changes a note rating from bad to good.

SOLUTION: The teacher and family should exchange telephone numbers in order to verify the ratings. If the student forges a rating, the consequence should be the loss of a privilege as described above.

·············· *Scenario 3* ··············

PROBLEM: There is a substitute teacher, and the student is unsure of how to get a rating.

SOLUTION: Written instructions can be left in a special folder for substitutes. Or the student can be taught to go to the office at the end of the school day and ask an office aide to help get the rating from the substitute.

TECHNIQUE TIP

Write the instructions for the student to follow in this situation on the note in the "Comments" section. ~

·············· *Scenario 4* ··············

PROBLEM: The student refuses to take the note altogether.

SOLUTION: This rarely happens. But if the student totally rejects taking the note or destroys it, use the same consequences as for a lost note. These consequences can be given both at home and at school until the student complies.

·············· *Scenario 5* ··············

PROBLEM: The student argues with you about a rating.

SOLUTION: Tell the student that if she continues to argue, an even lower rating will be given or a note will be written to her family in the "Comments" section about the inappropriate arguing.

TECHNIQUE TIP

It helps to call the family after an episode of arguing to make sure the note made it home. ~

·············· *Scenario 6* ··············

PROBLEM: The family offers extremely large rewards with too long of a time period before they are delivered (e.g., a bicycle, four-wheeler, a trip, a remote-control toy, large sums of money).

SOLUTION: Talk to the family and express your concern about the promised large reward. Help them compile a list of smaller rewards to be given within a much shorter time period and suggest the large reward as an additional **bonus.**

·············· *Scenario 7* ··············

PROBLEM: The family is incapable of delivering positive reinforcement and mild reductive consequences at home.

SOLUTION: Try putting together a reinforcer kit that contains simple rewards (e.g., candy, stickers, school supplies) and deliver it to the home so the family can use it for good notes. If they agree to review the note but still don't use the prepared kit, give the rewards from the kit in the classroom when the student returns the note the following day. If the family is incapable of applying mild reductive consequences at home,

discuss dropping the reductive consequences at home and instead apply them at school.

·············· *Scenario 8* ··············

PROBLEM: The student's family refuses to participate in the Home Note program and will not even sign the note.

SOLUTION: Ask the family for a face-to-face meeting in which you discuss the problem with them. Make the meeting positive, and try to respond to their concerns. It helps to appeal to the person who seems most willing to participate and work with you. Explain that the note is not designed to punish the student, but rather give the student feedback about his behavior and performance. Emphasize the idea of cooperation between the home and school and how this will maximally benefit the student. Ask the family if they are willing to try the program for as little as two weeks. If they still refuse, indicate that you would like to give the student the note anyway and hope they will look at the note. In this case, you will need to apply the positive reinforcement and reductive consequences at school.

TECHNIQUE TIP

Make sure the note is mostly positive during this trial period of time. ~

"Emphasize cooperation between the home and school and how this will maximally benefit the student."

.... *Scenario 9* ....

PROBLEM: You suspect that the family may emotionally or physically abuse the student if she receives a poor performance rating on the note.

SOLUTION: Invite the family to come in for a meeting and ask for their cooperation in making the Home Note program positive. Indicate that you want to downplay the reductive consequences. Tell the family that if they punish too much and reward too little, the student will learn to dislike both the program and school. If you suspect the abuse is continuing, you may have to call the authorities. This is a serious problem, but it rarely occurs.

.... *Scenario 10* ....

PROBLEM: The student insists he is responsible, does not need a Home Note, and wants to be off the program.

SOLUTION: Indicate to the student that he may, in fact, be responsible. However, one way to show responsibility is to do well with the Home Note. Develop a contract with the student. For example, when the student has good daily notes for four weeks, switch him to a weekly note that is rated on Fridays. When the student has four good weekly notes in a row, take him off the program for a trial period. However, indicate that if the student's behavior or performance slips, the weekly note system will be resumed.

Making Home Notes Even Better

1 Combining the Home Notes with the 30-item behavioral checklist will improve the performance of the Home Note program

(see the "Importance of Classroom Behavior [Teacher Rating Form]" at the end of this section and the picture icons [see Reproducible 2-1] provided in this section's reproducible tools). Rate the 30-item behavioral checklist for the student. Pick three to five of the behaviors rated as most important to you and the family. Use these items as the target behaviors to rate for the Home Note.

Each item in the checklist has a corresponding picture icon (e.g., picture icon #7 corresponds to behavioral checklist item #7, etc.). Each picture icon actually depicts the appropriate behavior for the checklist item. To use the picture icons, write the behavioral definition from the checklist on the Home Note, cut out its corresponding picture icon, and paste it on the note (see Figure 2-1). You can do this the old-fashioned way with a copier and scissors, or you can electronically cut and paste using the electronic version of these forms found on the CD. See the "Using the CD" file on the CD for more detailed directions. You may have to reduce the size of some of the picture icons to make them fit on the Home Note. After a note is made with the pasted icons, make several copies of the note and keep the original.

2 When selecting the behaviors for the Home Note, it is most effective to also include some academic subjects to be rated (e.g., reading, arithmetic, writing, etc.). An "all behavior" or an "all academic subject" note is less effective.

3 For secondary students, use the note titled "Information Note," Reproducibles 2-4a and 2-4b (see Figure 2-2). This note has seven areas for seven periods in a junior high or high school. The subjects and teachers' names should be written in each space in the order that the student attends classes. The

"Information Note" can be either a daily or a weekly note. For a weekly note, write "Weekly" in the blank space in the upper left hand corner. For a daily note, staple five notes together and write "MON" in this space for the first note, "TUE" for the next note, and so on for the whole week.

The "Information Note" can also be used with elementary students. It is particularly useful because it includes spaces for assigned homework, upcoming tests, and missing work.

Both Spanish and English versions of all REPRODUCIBLE TOOLS appear on the CD.

Figure 2-2

Figure 2-1

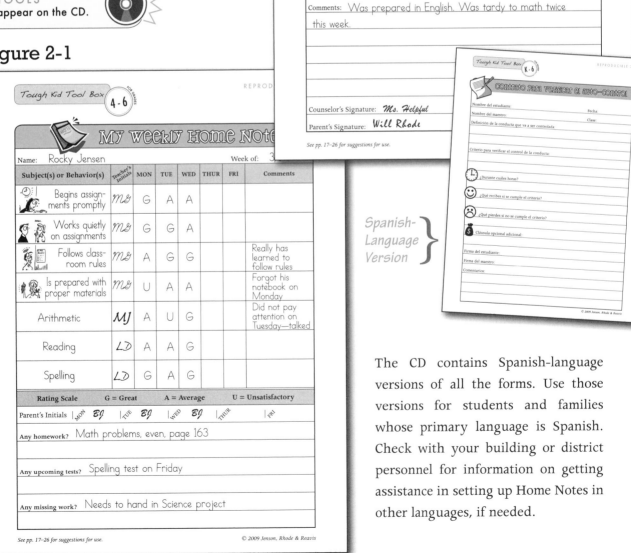

Spanish-Language Version

The CD contains Spanish-language versions of all the forms. Use those versions for students and families whose primary language is Spanish. Check with your building or district personnel for information on getting assistance in setting up Home Notes in other languages, if needed.

4 **Complete the Home Note with the Mystery Motivator program** (see Section 1 of this book and Chapter 2 of *The Tough Kid Book*). For each day that the student returns the note signed by her parent(s), she gets to color in a Mystery Motivator square.

5 **Let the student save good Home Notes for a behavioral contract reward.** For example, when the student has three good weeks of signed Home Notes, he is allowed a special treat (e.g., lunch with the teacher, selecting a video for the class to watch, a popcorn party, etc.).

> ⚠️ **CAUTION**
>
> Allow the student to collect notes cumulatively (e.g., the student may have two good weeks, a poor week, and then a good week) for the contract. A consecutive contract (e.g., three weeks of good Home Notes in a row) is an inappropriate and punishing criterion.

6 **Use a random Home Note program with the whole class.** Send an explanation sheet to all families of the students in your class indicating that sometimes (randomly) a Home Note will be sent home to inform them of their child's classroom behavior and performance on that day. During the week (on different days) pick four of five students and send a Home Note home with them. It helps to include the classroom rules in addition to the rated behavior items and a general category for academic performance for the family's reference.

Tell the students that you will be calling one or two of their families to inform them that the note is coming home. Also, require the students to return the notes signed by a family member. Random notes across the week for students are more effective than a fixed note sent home on Fridays.

> ⚠️ **CAUTION**
>
> Make this a primarily positive program, and do not threaten students that if they do not behave, you will send a bad note home.

 *TECHNIQUE TIP*

Select students at random for a Home Note by picking their names out of a container. ~

Importance of Classroom Behaviors
(Teacher Rating Form)

Please rate how important it is to you that a student do the following items:	Not important	Somewhat important	Moderately important	Quite important	Extremely important
I. Classroom Behavior					
The student:					
1. Listens quietly to directions	1	2	3	4	5
2. Follows oral directions accurately	1	2	3	4	5
3. Follows written directions accurately	1	2	3	4	5
4. Appears attentive during discussions	1	2	3	4	5
5. Is prepared with proper materials	1	2	3	4	5
6. Begins assignments promptly	1	2	3	4	5
7. Works quietly on assignments	1	2	3	4	5
8. Asks for help when needed, but not to excess	1	2	3	4	5
9. Turns in assignments on time	1	2	3	4	5
10. Follows classroom rules	1	2	3	4	5
11. Completes assigned tasks	1	2	3	4	5
II. Basic Interaction Skills					
The student:					
12. Contributes appropriately to discussions	1	2	3	4	5
13. Is responsive to the teacher's praise and attention	1	2	3	4	5
14. Engages in conversations appropriately	1	2	3	4	5
15. Makes requests appropriately	1	2	3	4	5
III. Getting Along Skills					
The student:					
16. Participates in group activities	1	2	3	4	5
17. Follows rules on the playground	1	2	3	4	5
18. Follows rules in hallways and bathrooms	1	2	3	4	5
19. Is positive and friendly	1	2	3	4	5

Importance of Classroom Behaviors
(Teacher Rating Form)

	Not important	Somewhat important	Moderately important	Quite important	Extremely important
III. Getting Along Skills *(continued)*					
The student:					
20. Is cooperative	1	2	3	4	5
21. Gets the teacher's attention appropriately	1	2	3	4	5
22. Gets his or her peers' attention appropriately	1	2	3	4	5
23. Gets along with others on the playground	1	2	3	4	5
IV. Coping Skills					
The student:					
24. Expresses anger appropriately	1	2	3	4	5
25. Uses appropriate language (no swearing)	1	2	3	4	5
26. Enjoys competition in the classroom/on the playground	1	2	3	4	5
27. Resists peer pressure	1	2	3	4	5
28. Disagrees appropriately	1	2	3	4	5
29. Accepts "no" for an answer	1	2	3	4	5
30. Accepts criticism or consequences appropriately	1	2	3	4	5

Tough Kid Tool Box

Home Note Reproducible Tools

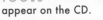

Both Spanish and English versions of all REPRODUCIBLE TOOLS appear on the CD.

Cut and Paste Icons for Home Notes

These picture icons correspond to the numbered items on the "Importance of Classroom Behaviors (Teaching Rating Form)" in Chapter 2.

Countoons adapted with permission by the Children's Behavior Therapy Unit's Generalization Project. Countoon drawings by Tom Oling.

See pp. 17–26 for suggestions for use.

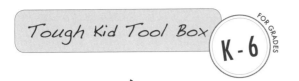

MY Daily Home Note

Name: _____   Date: _____

Parent's Initials						

Behavior(s)	Teacher's Initials	MON	TUE	WED	THUR	FRI

Rating Scale	Unsatisfactory = 1	Average = 2	Great = 3

Comments: _____
_____
_____
_____
_____

Teacher's Phone: _____   Student's Home Phone: _____

See pp. 17–26 for suggestions for use.   © 2009 Jenson, Rhode & Reavis

Tough Kid Tool Box   FOR GRADES   K-6

MY WEEKLY HOME NOTE

Name: _____   Week of: _____

Subject(s) or Behavior(s)	Teacher's Initials	MON	TUE	WED	THUR	FRI	Comments

Rating Scale	G = Great	A = Average	U = Unsatisfactory

Parent's Initials | MON | TUE | WED | THUR | FRI

Any homework?

Any upcoming tests?

Any missing work?

See pp. 17–26 for suggestions for use.

Information Note

Name: Date/Week of: Phone:

Periods	Teacher's Initials	Class Performance (circle one)	Assigned Homework	Upcoming Tests?	Missing Work?
		G Great A Average U Unsatisfactory			
		G Great A Average U Unsatisfactory			
		G Great A Average U Unsatisfactory			
		G Great A Average U Unsatisfactory			
		G Great A Average U Unsatisfactory			
		G Great A Average U Unsatisfactory			
		G Great A Average U Unsatisfactory			

Comments:

Counselor's Signature:

Parent's Signature:

See pp. 17–26 for suggestions for use.

Information Note

Name: **Date/Week of:**   **Phone:**

Periods	Teacher's Initials	Class Performance (circle one)	Assigned Homework	Upcoming Tests?	Missing Work?
		G Great A Average U Unsatisfactory			
		G Great A Average U Unsatisfactory			
		G Great A Average U Unsatisfactory			
		G Great A Average U Unsatisfactory			
		G Great A Average U Unsatisfactory			
		G Great A Average U Unsatisfactory			
		G Great A Average U Unsatisfactory			

Rating Scale   Great = _____   Average = _____   Unsatisfactory = _____

Comments:

Self-Monitoring Programs

def•i•ni•tion

Self-monitoring is a process in which the student observes and collects data on his or her own behavior. Monitoring one's own behavior is an important part of self-management.

de•scrip•tion

Self-monitoring programs are effective for changing many types of tough behaviors. The student is given a recording form and instructed to mark down each time that a pre-specified behavior occurs. The very act of marking down and keeping track of the behavior will often by itself change how often the behavior occurs. Disruptive behaviors generally decrease and appropriate behaviors increase when they are self-monitored. Good self-monitoring programs include well-defined behaviors, an easy-to-use recording form, and rewards.

Steps for Implementing a Self-Monitoring Program

STEP 1 Determine the specific behavior that the student is to self-monitor. Self-monitoring may be effectively used to reduce behaviors such as talk-outs, not following the classroom rules, tardiness, and being off task. Behaviors to increase could include studying independently, following the classroom rules, completing assignments on time, remaining in one's seat, and raising one's hand to talk.

TECHNIQUE TIP

The 30-item behavioral checklist used to select target behaviors for intervention with Home Notes can also be used for self-monitoring. (See the "Importance of Classroom Behaviors [Teacher Rating Form]" in Section 2 of this book.). ~

STEP 2 Select an appropriate recording form for the student to use. (Several forms—Reproducibles 3-1 through 3-3—are provided in this section's reproducible tools.)

STEP 3 Define the target behavior for the student and include several examples. It is usually better to have the student record only one behavior at a time. The exception may be having the student record how well she is following the classroom rules.

TECHNIQUE TIP

It may help to model the behavior so the student understands exactly what she should be recording. ~

 STEP 4 Define the time period in which you want the student to self-monitor the behavior. It is better to give the student a specific time, such as during math period, at recess, or during the first half of the day.

TECHNIQUE TIP

It is best not to use short recording intervals such as ten-second intervals because they are too complex and frequent for the student to monitor. It is much easier to have the student record the behavior: (1) each time the behavior occurs, such as a talk-out, or (2) when she thinks of it (e.g., "In history class, record a mark when you realize you are on task and studying."). ~

 STEP 5 Give the student the recording form for a trial run during the time period in which you want him to self-monitor.

TECHNIQUE TIP

You may need to prompt the student to record the behavior during this period. If the student talks out and does not mark it down, tell him to mark it down. It is also important to prompt the student to mark down appropriate behaviors as well as inappropriate ones. (For example, "Tameka, you are studying. Please mark it down on your sheet."). ~

 STEP 6 At the end of a recording period, have the student write down the actual number of target behavior occurrences on a summary sheet. A "Weekly Summary Sheet" is included in this section's reproducible tools for this purpose.

STEP 7 Self-monitoring will change a behavior only temporarily. To make the change permanent, it helps to tie the self-monitoring program to some type of contingency. For example, if the student keeps his talk-outs below two during a specified time period, he may earn a small reward or privilege. The contingencies may be gradually withdrawn over time. However, you should continue to praise the student's appropriate behavior.

TECHNIQUE TIP

Use Mystery Motivators (see Section 1 of this book and Chapter 2 of *The Tough Kid Book*) or Spinners as rewards for the self-monitoring program. ~

Troubleshooting Self-Monitoring

.... *Scenario 1* ....

PROBLEM: The student refuses to self-monitor the behavior.

SOLUTION: Offer the student an incentive or reward for using the program. If the student still refuses, a classroom privilege like recess can be linked to program use.

.... *Scenario 2* ....

PROBLEM: The student keeps missing occurrences of the behavior to record.

SOLUTION: When the behavior occurs and is missed, point it out to the student and prompt her to record it. Check your definition of the behavior to be recorded with what the student thinks she should be recording. Make sure the definition is specific, and if necessary, model the behavior. It may also help to have the student sit near you so that you can easily prompt her.

.... *Scenario 3* ....

PROBLEM: The student cheats in recording her behavior.

SOLUTION: Tell the student that you may also be recording her behavior. If your total does not closely match hers, a reward will be missed or a privilege will be lost.

Making Self-Monitoring Even Better

1 The more outstanding, creative, or unique the recording technique, the bigger the behavior change will generally be. However, the procedure should not be so intrusive that a student becomes embarrassed. Recording instruments may include a golf counter, sewing stitch counter, or a small hand calculator where the number one is added to get a total or sum each time a behavior occurs.

TECHNIQUE TIP

Pictures that represent the behavior help make the recording procedure unique. Use the picture icons (see Reproducible 2-1) provided in Section 2 of this book on the recording sheet, or make up cartoon icons of your own. ~

2 The changes that occur when a student starts to self-monitor are temporary. They will fade with time unless they are combined with rewards. For example, if a student is self-monitoring her classroom rule-breaking behavior, make the student eligible for a Mystery Motivator drawing if she breaks less than one rule per day. Always combine the reward with social praise. For example, "What a great contribution; you are really following the classroom rules. It is a joy to have you in class!" As the frequency of the reward is gradually reduced over time, social praise for the appropriate behavior will help to maintain it.

TECHNIQUE TIP

Combine the reward with a formal written contract from this section's reproducible tools or from Section 4 (Behavioral Contracting). Section 4 provides an in-depth explanation of the effective use of contracting. ~

3 Have the student summarize his self-monitoring information each day on a summary sheet. It helps to use a summary sheet that has spaces for the Best Daily Score and the Weekly Average, like the "Weekly Summary Sheet" provided in this section's reproducible tools. These results can also be graphed by the student; however, it is important to keep the graphing simple.

4 Matching the student's self-monitored results with your recording of the behavior is an excellent way to improve the procedure and make a student more aware of the perceptions of others. Self-monitoring and matching to your results should be simple.

It is also important to remember that recording matches will not always be exact. An exact match should not be required.

TECHNIQUE TIP

See Reproducibles 3-4 and 3-5 for a simple method of recording how well the student's self-monitoring matches your evaluation. A single line through the student's rating indicates a match (agreement with the teacher's rating. An "X" through the student's rating indicates a mismatch (disagreement). Count the number of Xs on the form and compare with the total number of ratings to determine whether there is a significant mismatch between the student's perception and yours.~

5   **A well-designed self-monitoring program should include very specific behaviors that are beneficial to both the teacher and student.** The first program we suggest for Tough Kids is self-monitoring their compliance with the classroom rules. This is done by listing the rules on the self-monitoring form and recording them for the morning and afternoon sessions. A "Monitoring Classroom Rules" form (Reproducible 3-4) is provided in this section's reproducible tools for this purpose. It helps to compare the student's recording with your counts.

Self-monitoring is also helpful for other common behaviors, including talk-outs and disturbing others. A "Monitoring Talk-Outs" form (Reproducible 3-3) and a "Monitoring Behavior Form" (Reproducible 3-5) are provided in this section's reproducible tools for this purpose.

Similarly, self-monitoring can be used with academic behaviors such as handing in assignments, staying on task, working independently, and turning in homework. An "On Task/Working Monitoring Form" (Reproducible 3-2) is provided in this section's reproducible tools.

6   **Improvements in behavior can be greatly enhanced when teams of students self-monitor their behavior.** For example, three-member teams might record who completed and the correctness of their homework assignments. The results can be recorded on team summary sheets as averages.

"The first program we suggest for Tough Kids is self-monitoring their compliance with the classroom rules."

Tough Kid Tool Box

Self-Monitoring Reproducible Tools

Both Spanish and English versions of all REPRODUCIBLE TOOLS appear on the CD.

© 2009 Jenson, Rhode & Reavis

Contract for Self-Monitoring

Student's Name: _____ Date: _____

Teacher's Name: _____ Class: _____

Definition of Behavior to Be Monitored:

Criterion for Monitored Behavior:

Over What Time?

What do you get if the criterion is met?

What do you lose if the criterion is not met?

Optional Bonus Clause:

Signature of Student:

Signature of Teacher:

Comments:

See pp. 33–36 for suggestions for use.

On Task/Working Monitoring Form

Student's Name: _____

Date: _____   Class: _____

+ 0

1.															
2.															
3.															
4.															
5.															
6.															
7.															
8.															
9.															
10.															

Instructions for Using the Monitoring Form

When you are in class and think about it, put a "+" in a square if you are working or studying. Put a "0" in a square if you are off task and not working.

Fill in row 1 first and then row 2, and so on. You should fill in at least two rows per class.

Comments: _____

Tough Kid Tool Box

K - 6 FOR GRADES

MOnitOring Talk-Outs

Student's Name: _____   Date: _____

Teacher's Name: _____   Class: _____

Times	Number of Talk-Outs This Hour	Teacher's Comments

Definition of a Talk-Out:

_____

_____

_____

Correct Way to Talk in Class:

_____

_____

_____

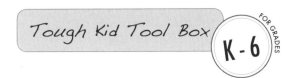

Tough Kid Tool Box

K-6 FOR GRADES

MONITORING CLASSROOM RULES

Student's Name: _____   Date: _____

Teacher's Name: _____   Class: _____

Classroom Rules	Morning	Afternoon
	1 2 3 4	1 2 3 4
	1 2 3 4	1 2 3 4
	1 2 3 4	1 2 3 4
	1 2 3 4	1 2 3 4
	1 2 3 4	1 2 3 4
	1 2 3 4	1 2 3 4
	1 2 3 4	1 2 3 4
	1 2 3 4	1 2 3 4

Rating Scale—Circle a Number

1 = Needs Improvement   2 = Barely OK   3 = Average   4 = Great

If the teacher agrees with the student rating, put a line across the circled rating. ⊘

If the teacher disagrees with the student rating, put an "X" across the circled rating. ⊗

Comments:

See pp. 33–36 for suggestions for use.   © 2009 Jenson, Rhode & Reavis

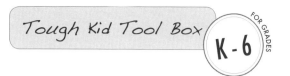

Monitoring Behavior Form

Student's Name: _____ Date: _____

Teacher's Name: _____ Class: _____

Periods	Performance Rating	Teacher's Comments
	1 2 3 4	
	1 2 3 4	
	1 2 3 4	
	1 2 3 4	
	1 2 3 4	
	1 2 3 4	
	1 2 3 4	
	1 2 3 4	

Rating Scale—Circle a Number

1 = Needs Improvement   2 = Barely OK   3 = Average   4 = Great

If the teacher agrees with the student rating, put a line across the circled rating. ⊘

If the teacher disagrees with the student rating, put an "X" across the circled rating. ⊗

Behavior(s) Being Rated:

_____

_____

_____

_____

See pp. 33–36 for suggestions for use.

weekly Summary Sheet

Student's Name: _____   Date: _____

Best Daily Score: _____   Weekly Average: _____

Self-Monitored Behaviors		MON	TUE	WED	THUR	FRI
1.	A.M.					
	P.M.					
2.	A.M.					
	P.M.					
3.	A.M.					
	P.M.					

INSTRUCTIONS

1. Define one to three behaviors and write them in the boxes.
2. Have the student record the behaviors for the morning and the afternoon each weekday.
3. Do not have the student keep track of more than three behaviors.
4. Have the student write his or her best daily score and weekly average at the top of the form.

Comments: _____

_____

_____

Behavioral Contracting

def•i•ni•tion

Contracting involves placing contingencies for reinforcement into a written document that is agreed to and signed by the student, the teacher, and any other individuals who are involved with the contract. Contracts may be effectively used with students of all ages to increase desired behaviors or decrease undesired ones.

de•scrip•tion

When adults see the word *contract*, they generally think of corporate mergers or sports stars signing agreements for millions of dollars. Contracts also have everyday meaning for most adults in terms of buying or renting cars, getting married, and business and employment agreements. Contracts are used in conjunction with many adult behaviors because they are explicit and set expectations. For similar reasons, contracts can also be used effectively when working with Tough Kids. (See Reproducibles 4-1 through 4-13.)

Steps for Implementing Behavioral Contracting

 Define the specific behavior for which the contract is being implemented.

Poor examples include "improving classroom responsibility" and "showing respect for authority." Poor examples are vague and/or judgmental.

Better examples include "hand in work by the end of the period without being asked" and "talk in a calm voice to classmates with no arguing." Good examples are descriptive, specific pinpoints of behavior.

TECHNIQUE TIP

Break the initial contract behavior into smaller steps, if necessary, so that the student will be successful. It is important for the student to be successful in earning the contract reinforcer so that she will be motivated to continue. ~

STEP 2 Select the contract rein- forcers with the help of the student.

TECHNIQUE TIP

Reinforcers should not take a lot of time to deliver, nor should they be expensive. ~

STEP 3 Define the contract criteria— including the amount of the behavior required, the amount of reinforcement to be provided, and the time limits for performance.

TECHNIQUE TIP

Cumulative criteria are usually preferable to consecutive criteria. Cumulative criteria allow the student to make mistakes (some periods of not meeting the criteria) without having to start over from the beginning. Consecutive criteria can be very discouraging for the student. ~

STEP 4 If necessary, include a "bonus clause" for exceptional performance or behavior completed before the contract time limits. Consider adding a "penalty clause" for nonperformance if the initial contract does not work even though the rewards are valued and the payoff time is short.

"Indicate that the target behavior, rewards, and criteria are negotiable."

STEP 5 Negotiate the contract with the student:

- Indicate why a contract is necessary and that you want to help.
- Discuss the target behavior, reinforcement (rewards), and performance criteria.
- Indicate that the target behavior, rewards, and criteria are negotiable. Emphasize, however, that a contract is needed and its implementation is not negotiable.
- Tell the student what you suggest in these areas. Ask for the student's input.
- Don't allow the student to set unrealistically high standards for herself. Encourage the student to begin slowly and then expand.
- Indicate that a "penalty clause" may be necessary, if applicable.
- Indicate that the contract may need to be renegotiated at some point in the future.

STEP 6 Put the terms of the con- tract in writing.

TECHNIQUE TIP

Writing and signing a contract prevents misunderstandings and indicates agreement with the terms at the time that all the participating parties sign the contract. ~

STEP 7 Set a date for reviewing (and possibly renegotiating) the contract.

STEP 8 Have all participating par- ties sign the contract. Keep a copy, and make a copy for each of the participants.

Troubleshooting Behavioral Contracting

.... *Scenario 1* ....

PROBLEM: The student begins by working hard and then loses motivation.

SOLUTION: The reward payoff may be too delayed. Cut the time period in half. Delaying the reward too long is one of the most frequent problems with contracting.

.... *Scenario 2* ....

PROBLEM: The student appears confused and never really gets started.

SOLUTION: The required behavior may not be defined or explained clearly enough, or too much of the required behavior may be expected initially. Discuss the expectations thoroughly with the student. If necessary, model and role-play the target behavior. If the student understands the requirement but is still not performing, the requirement may be too great. Try reducing the behavior requirement for one week (half the problems, half the points, etc.). After the student has received the contract reward at least once, gradually begin to increase the contract requirement again.

.... *Scenario 3* ....

PROBLEM: The student is still unmotivated and disinterested, even after the teacher has shortened the delay in earning the reward, clarified the student's understanding of the expectations, and the student has earned the contract reward at least once.

SOLUTION: A penalty clause may be needed to prompt the student to actively participate.

.... *Scenario 4* ....

PROBLEM: The student was excited to start the contract in the beginning, but now appears frustrated and anxious.

SOLUTION: Check the performance criteria. Student frustration can result from expectations that are too difficult. Be sure to use cumulative criteria rather than consecutive criteria.

.... *Scenario 5* ....

PROBLEM: The student is openly defiant and will not participate in contracting.

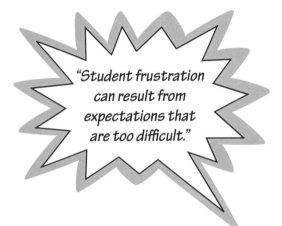

"Student frustration can result from expectations that are too difficult."

SOLUTION: Indicate to the student that you want to negotiate the terms of the contract and value the student's input. If possible, invite an adult who is important to the student to participate in the negotiations, especially if a penalty clause is set. This person may be a parent, a coach, a favorite teacher, a counselor, etc. Make certain beforehand, however, that the invited person supports the idea of a contract.

Making Behavioral Contracting Even Better

The following points are helpful in ensuring that the behavioral contract effects change in the student:

■ **Agreeing:** You must negotiate the consequences and reinforcement for specific behaviors with the student.

TECHNIQUE TIP

Negotiations should not be one-sided in the sense that you dictate the terms to the student and the student signs them. ~

■ **Formal Exchange:** The reward is always given **after** the behavior is produced. You must not relax the behavior requirements at any point in the contract period once it has begun.

■ **Behavior:** The target behavior must be specifically and objectively defined, including an expected standard (e.g., 80% or better) and time deadlines (e.g., by 3:30 P.M. next Friday) for performance.

■ **Goal Setting:** Contracting and goal setting can be combined to assist the student in setting her own goals. A penalty clause and bonus clause may also be useful with goal setting.

■ **Advertising for Success:** Contracting for performance improvement can be developed and then the improvements publicly posted. (See Section 7 of this book for additional information on the Advertising for Success program.)

■ **Group Contingencies:** Contracts can be developed for the whole classroom or for student teams within the classroom. The procedures are basically the same as for contracting with an individual student.

TECHNIQUE TIP

The teacher must be certain that each student in the class or on a team is capable of meeting the contract expectations. ~

■ **Home Notes:** Contracting can be used in combination with Home Notes (see Section 2 of this book and Chapter 4 of *The Tough Kid Book,* 2nd ed.). When a student has accumulated a certain number of acceptable Home Notes, the agreed-upon (contracted) reward will be delivered.

■ **Level System Contracts:** A more sophisticated contract, a "level system" contract can be used to help shape students' desired behavior over a period of time by automatically adjusting their access to privileges based on how well they meet classroom expectations during the contracting period. Access to privileges at home, in the classroom, or a combination of the two may be incorporated into this intervention.

The level system contracts in this section's reproducible tools contain the following components:

• A rating form that includes each school day of the week. One example (Reproducible 4-10) has suggested potential expectations, and the other (Reproducible 4-11) may be tailored for individual student needs.

• The actual contract form (Reproducible 4-12) to be discussed with the student, mutually agreed upon, and signed by both the student and teacher

• A level system contract privileges form (Reproducible 4-13) on which to write down agreed-upon privileges the student can earn by meeting the specified criteria (e.g., at least three "Excellents" and two "OKs" for Level 3 privileges).

It is suggested that initial level system contracts be written for a week at a time, with ratings tallied on Fridays to determine privileges for the coming week. To maximize the effects of the system, an additional daily reward may be added for specific ratings. For example, the student may earn a desired treat for an "Excellent" rating, a sticker for an "OK" rating, and no reward for a "Poor" rating.

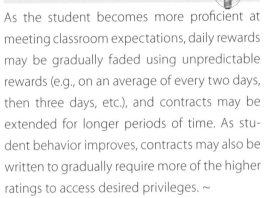

TECHNIQUE TIP

As the student becomes more proficient at meeting classroom expectations, daily rewards may be gradually faded using unpredictable rewards (e.g., on an average of every two days, then three days, etc.), and contracts may be extended for longer periods of time. As student behavior improves, contracts may also be written to gradually require more of the higher ratings to access desired privileges. ~

Cautions With Behavioral Contracting

Teachers should remember that most contracts in life operate with a delayed reward "payoff" system. But when you are working with Tough Kids, delays frequently destroy the initial steps that are required to get them started. Contracts used with Tough Kids are most effective when: (1) they are used as a way of fading out more frequent rewards or after a student has begun to perform appropriately, or (2) they are used with older or more motivated students. Contracts with long delays will be ineffective for younger or highly unmotivated students. In these cases, it is better to start with an hourly, twice daily, or daily reward system.

Behavioral Contracting Reproducible Tools

Both Spanish and English versions of all REPRODUCIBLE TOOLS appear on the CD.

Amazing Turtles Leaping Hurdles

I, _____, agree to _____

_____ during _____

time. If I am successful, then I may color in a turtle. When all five of the turtles are

colored in, I will get _____.

Date _____

Student _____

Teacher _____

Achiever Beaver Contract

I, _____, agree to _____

_____ during _____

time. If I am successful, then I may color in a beaver. When all five of the beavers are

colored in, I will get _____.

Date _____

Student _____

Teacher _____

See pp. 45–49 for suggestions for use.

Tough Kid Tool Box

FOR GRADES
K-6

Bus Contract

Student Name _____

Ride to School (date/day) _____   ❏ Excellent ❏ OK ❏ Poor

Ride Home (date/day) _____   ❏ Excellent ❏ OK ❏ Poor

Target Behaviors: 1. _____

2. _____

3. _____

If I earn _____ (#) Excellents, _____ (#) OKs, or _____ (#) Poors, I will get _____

_____. If I earn _____ (#) Excellents,

_____ (#) OKs, or _____ (#) Poors, I will lose _____

_____.

Comments:_____

_____

Bus Contract

Student Name _____

Ride to School (date/day) _____   ❏ Excellent ❏ OK ❏ Poor

Ride Home (date/day) _____   ❏ Excellent ❏ OK ❏ Poor

Target Behaviors: 1. _____

2. _____

3. _____

If I earn _____ (#) Excellents, _____ (#) OKs, or _____ (#) Poors, I will get _____

_____. If I earn _____ (#) Excellents,

_____ (#) OKs, or _____ (#) Poors, I will lose _____

_____.

Comments:_____

_____

See pp. 45–49 for suggestions for use.   © 2009 Jenson, Rhode & Reavis

Bus Contract

Student Name _____

Ride to School (date/day) _____ ➜

Ride Home (date/day) _____ ➜

Point Rating		
Outstanding	OK	Poor
5 4	3	2 1
5 4	3	2 1

Target Behaviors:

1. _____

2. _____

3. _____

If I earn _____ (#) points, then I will receive _____.

Comments: _____

_____

Rated by: _____

Bus Contract

Student Name _____

Ride to School (date/day) _____ ➜

Ride Home (date/day) _____ ➜

Point Rating		
Outstanding	OK	Poor
5 4	3	2 1
5 4	3	2 1

Target Behaviors:

1. _____

2. _____

3. _____

If I earn _____ (#) points, then I will receive _____.

Comments: _____

_____

Rated by: _____

See pp. 45–49 for suggestions for use.

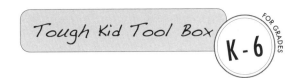

Bus Ride

Ride to School (date/day) _____ (5 points possible)

Ride Home (date/day) _____ (5 points possible)

TARGET BEHAVIORS

Student Names	1. Stay in Seat	2. Talk Quietly	3. Follow Directions	4.	5.	6.	7.	To School Points	Going Home Points

Comments A.M. Ride: _____

_____

Comments P.M. Ride: _____

_____

Rated by _____

(Signature or Initials/Position)

See pp. 45–49 for suggestions for use.   © 2009 Jenson, Rhode & Reavis

Lunchroom Contract

Behavior

Who _____

What   1. _____

            2. _____

            3._____

When _____

How Well _____

Sign here. _____   _____

                           (Student)   (Date)

                           _____   _____

                           (Teacher)   (Date)

Lunchroom Record: "+" = Criteria Met, "0" = Criteria Not Met				
MONDAY	**TUESDAY**	**WEDNESDAY**	**THURSDAY**	**FRIDAY**

Reward

Given by _____

What _____

When _____

How Much _____

See pp. 45–49 for suggestions for use.

Class Lunchroom Contract

We, the undersigned, agree to perform the following behaviors in the lunchroom:

1. _____   3. _____   5. _____

2. _____   4. _____   6. _____

We will perform these behaviors for the contract period from _____ to

_____ . As a reward, we will receive _____

on _____

Student Signatures:

_____   _____   _____

_____   _____   _____

_____   _____   _____

_____   _____   _____

_____   _____   _____

_____   _____   _____

_____   _____   _____

_____   _____   _____

_____   _____   _____

The teacher agrees to see that the reward is carried out.

_____   _____
(Teacher Signature)   (Date)

See pp. 45–49 for suggestions for use.

© 2009 Jenson, Rhode & Reavis

Homework Contract

I, _____, agree to complete the homework assignment(s) for the following subjects:

1. _____   4. _____

2. _____   5. _____

3. _____   6. _____

with at least _____% accuracy in _____ out of _____ subjects over a time period of
(Number)   (Number)

_____ to _____.
(Date)   (Date)

· ·

For meeting criteria on _____ out of _____ days, I can earn _____
(Number)   (Number)

_____ to be delivered _____ by _____.
(When)   (Person)

CONTRACT

_____   _____
(Student Signature)   (Date)

_____   _____
(Teacher Signature)   (Date)

See pp. 45–49 for suggestions for use.

© 2009 Jenson, Rhode & Reavis

RECESS Contract

Who _____   Date _____

What to Do: What **NOT** to Do:

1. _____   4. _____

2. _____   5. _____

3. _____   6. _____

. . . .

If I earn _____ (#/name of rating)

or better ratings during _____ time, I will receive _____

_____

to be provided by _____ on _____.

_____   _____
(Student Signature)   (Date)

_____   _____
(Teacher Signature)   (Date)

Morning Recess:

❏ Excellent   ❏ Good   ❏ OK   ❏ Poor

Lunch Recess:

❏ Excellent   ❏ Good   ❏ OK   ❏ Poor

Afternoon Recess:

❏ Excellent   ❏ Good   ❏ OK   ❏ Poor

See pp. 45–49 for suggestions for use.

Contract

I, _____, agree to do the following behaviors:

   1. _____

   2. _____

   3. _____

When: _____

How Well: _____

. . . .

If I am successful, I will receive_____,

given by _____ on _____.

Bonus Clause _____

_____

Penalty Clause _____

_____

_____   _____
(Student Signature)   (Date)

_____   _____
(Teacher Signature)   (Date)

See pp. 45–49 for suggestions for use.

Tough Kid Tool Box   K-6 FOR GRADES

Weekly Level System Contract With Key

Name: _____   Subject: _____   Week of: _____

MONDAY	Excellent ❑	OK ❑	Poor ❑	Teacher Signature _____	
Homework: Yes ❑ No ❑ If so, what?					
TUESDAY	Excellent ❑	OK ❑	Poor ❑	Teacher Signature _____	
Homework: Yes ❑ No ❑ If so, what?					
WEDNESDAY	Excellent ❑	OK ❑	Poor ❑	Teacher Signature _____	
Homework: Yes ❑ No ❑ If so, what?					
THURSDAY	Excellent ❑	OK ❑	Poor ❑	Teacher Signature _____	
Homework: Yes ❑ No ❑ If so, what?					
FRIDAY	Excellent ❑	OK ❑	Poor ❑	Teacher Signature _____	
Homework: Yes ❑ No ❑ If so, what?					

TOTALS FOR WEEK: Excellent _____   OK _____   Poor _____

Excellent	OK	Poor
1. On time	1. On time	1. Late
2. Consistently follows classroom rules	2. Follows classroom rules most of the time	2. Does not follow classroom rules
3. Completed assignments with 85–100% accuracy or worked consistently the entire period	3. Completed assignments with 65–85% accuracy	3. Completed assignments with less than 65% accuracy
4. Actively listens	4. Listens most of the time	4. Does not listen to the teacher
5. Volunteers in class discussions/activities	5. Participates when called upon	5. Does not participate in class discussions/activities

See pp. 45–49 for suggestions for use.

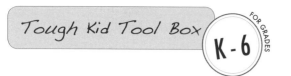

Weekly Level System Contract

Name: _____ Subject: _____ Week of: _____

MONDAY	Excellent ❑ OK ❑ Poor ❑ Teacher Signature _____
Homework: Yes ❑ No ❑ If so, what?	
TUESDAY	Excellent ❑ OK ❑ Poor ❑ Teacher Signature _____
Homework: Yes ❑ No ❑ If so, what?	
WEDNESDAY	Excellent ❑ OK ❑ Poor ❑ Teacher Signature _____
Homework: Yes ❑ No ❑ If so, what?	
THURSDAY	Excellent ❑ OK ❑ Poor ❑ Teacher Signature _____
Homework: Yes ❑ No ❑ If so, what?	
FRIDAY	Excellent ❑ OK ❑ Poor ❑ Teacher Signature _____
Homework: Yes ❑ No ❑ If so, what?	

TOTALS FOR WEEK: Excellent _____   OK _____   Poor _____

Excellent	OK	Poor
1.	1.	1.
2.	2.	2.
3.	3.	3.
4.	4.	4.
5.	5.	5.

See pp. 45–49 for suggestions for use.

Tough Kid Tool Box

Level System Contract

Contracting period: _____ to _____.

I, _____, agree to the following:

If I receive _____ Excellents

_____ OKs

_____ Poors

✸ I will earn **Level 1** privileges.

- -

If I receive _____ Excellents

_____ OKs

_____ Poors

✸ I will earn **Level 2** privileges.

- -

If I receive _____ Excellents

_____ OKs

_____ Poors

✸ I will earn **Level 3** privileges.

_____   _____
(Student Signature)   (Date)

_____   _____
(Teacher Signature)   (Date)

Level System Contract Privileges

Level 1 Privileges:

_____

_____

_____

_____

_____

Level 2 Privileges:

_____

_____

_____

_____

_____

Level 3 Privileges:

_____

_____

_____

_____

_____

Tracking Procedures

def•i•ni•tion

Tracking provides an effective means for teachers and other school staff to monitor students' behavior and academic performance in school settings other than their own.

de•scrip•tion

Tracking is particularly helpful for students who have multiple teachers during their school day and who require: (1) assistance in organizing their homework and/or (2) regular feedback on their performance. Monitoring student performance with tracking procedures allows for consistent, appropriate reinforcement for desired performance and corrective consequences for undesired performance in a timely fashion.

Steps for Implementing Tracking Procedures

STEP 1 Determine the academic or social behaviors for which monitoring using tracking forms is desired. Common tracking behaviors include following classroom rules, being on time to class, turning in completed homework, and participating appropriately in classroom activities. Determine the settings in which these behaviors take place.

STEP 2 Select a tracking form that incorporates the necessary behaviors and settings from this section's reproducible tools (Reproducibles 5-1 through 5-5b).

STEP 3 Communicate with the other school staff in the target settings about the need for their assistance in monitoring the student's performance. Com-municate with the student's family about the need for tracking at school. Discuss and determine with them whether the

"Tracking provides an effective means to monitor students' behavior."

tracking form will come home with the student on a regular basis or whether it will only be a method of communication among school staff regarding the student's performance.

STEP 4 Determine who will collect and review information from the tracking forms on a daily or weekly basis. Decide when this will take place (the time of day) and how. For example, the student may be asked to bring the tracking form to the attendance office or the special education teacher's room at the end of seventh period every day.

STEP 5 Select rewards for desirable performance and mild negative consequences for inadequate performance. Decide how well the student must perform to earn the rewards (e.g., no more than one missing homework assignment, no more than two classroom rules broken during the day) and what performance will earn the negative consequences (e.g., two or more homework assignments missing, three or more classroom rules broken during the day). Determine who will be providing the contingencies that the student has earned.

STEP 6 Review the tracking form and procedures with all participating adults (e.g., other school staff, the family) and secure their agreement to participate in the tracking program. Agree upon a starting date. Clarify to all concerned who will be collecting the forms from the student either daily or weekly.

STEP 7 Explain the tracking program to the student and secure his agreement to participate. Then implement the program.

STEP 8 Collect the tracking sheets from the student either daily or weekly, as previously determined.

STEP 9 Deliver rewards daily or weekly as agreed. Deliver mild negative consequences for: (1) not carrying the tracking form, (2) failing to have the teachers and/or family member sign the form, (3) losing the form, or (4) performance below agreed-upon criteria, if a penalty clause has been included.

STEP 10 Review the student's progress on a daily or weekly basis, depending on the terms of the contract. Meet with the student and/or other appropriate school staff to clarify questions and to discuss student progress.

STEP 11 Make any necessary adjustments to the tracking form or procedures, and re-implement the program.

STEP 12 As the tracking criteria are consistently met, gradually fade the checking of the tracking form to random, less frequent checks. Where possible, eventually fade out the tracking form altogether, encouraging the student to self-monitor (see Section 3 of this book).

Troubleshooting Tracking Procedures

PROBLEM: The student "loses" the tracking form, destroys it, or refuses to carry it.

SOLUTION: Add a penalty clause to the tracking procedures that will be delivered when these behaviors occur. Explain the penalty clause thoroughly to the student ahead of time.

PROBLEM: The student is missing one or more teacher's signatures or initials and says that the teacher didn't have time to mark and sign the form.

SOLUTION: Talk to the teachers in question and reemphasize the necessity of their taking the time to complete the form. Make certain they understand that the student will earn a penalty for an incomplete form. Notify the student that a penalty clause is being added, and implement it.

PROBLEM: The student is consistently not meeting the behavior performance criteria.

SOLUTION: Make certain that the student is capable of meeting the criteria and understands exactly what is expected. Review the problem areas with the student. Discuss why the problems are occurring (e.g., the student's homework was not completed because her book was lost or not taken home, the student was late to class because she always returns to her locker between every class, the student was talking in class because she was sitting next to a friend). Brainstorm ways to solve the problems and role-play the solutions with the student. Gain the student's commitment to correct the problem. If the student is unwilling to correct the problem, consider adding a penalty clause to the procedures that will be delivered when tracking criteria are not met.

Making Tracking Procedures Even Better

After implementing the tracking procedures successfully, teach the student to self-monitor his own performance. Gradually shift more and more responsibility for monitoring student performance from the participating adults to the student. (See Section 3 of this book for specific information and self-monitoring reproducible tools.)

"Gain the student's commitment to correct the problem."

Tracking Procedures Reproducible Tools

MYSTERY MOTIVATOR

CRAYONS

Both Spanish and English versions of all REPRODUCIBLE TOOLS appear on the CD.

© 2009 Jenson, Rhode & Reavis

Tough Kid Tool Box   FOR GRADES **6-12**

Student Tracking Form (by teacher)

Student Name: _____

Week of: _____

Instructions:

1. The student carries this form to each teacher daily.
2. Each teacher completes the rating and initials the form in the appropriate box at the end of class.
3. Additional teacher comments may be made on the back of this form.
4. The student reviews this form each day with _____, who initials the bottom row of this form.

Ratings:
G = Good
F = Fair
P = Poor

	Monday	Tuesday	Wednesday	Thursday	Friday
Period 1	Work G F P / Behavior G F P / Tardy ☐ / Homework:	Work G F P / Behavior G F P / Tardy ☐ / Homework:	Work G F P / Behavior G F P / Tardy ☐ / Homework:	Work G F P / Behavior G F P / Tardy ☐ / Homework:	Work G F P / Behavior G F P / Tardy ☐ / Homework:
Period 2	Work G F P / Behavior G F P / Tardy ☐ / Homework:	Work G F P / Behavior G F P / Tardy ☐ / Homework:	Work G F P / Behavior G F P / Tardy ☐ / Homework:	Work G F P / Behavior G F P / Tardy ☐ / Homework:	Work G F P / Behavior G F P / Tardy ☐ / Homework:
Period 3	Work G F P / Behavior G F P / Tardy ☐ / Homework:	Work G F P / Behavior G F P / Tardy ☐ / Homework:	Work G F P / Behavior G F P / Tardy ☐ / Homework:	Work G F P / Behavior G F P / Tardy ☐ / Homework:	Work G F P / Behavior G F P / Tardy ☐ / Homework:
Period 4	Work G F P / Behavior G F P / Tardy ☐ / Homework:	Work G F P / Behavior G F P / Tardy ☐ / Homework:	Work G F P / Behavior G F P / Tardy ☐ / Homework:	Work G F P / Behavior G F P / Tardy ☐ / Homework:	Work G F P / Behavior G F P / Tardy ☐ / Homework:
Period 5	Work G F P / Behavior G F P / Tardy ☐ / Homework:	Work G F P / Behavior G F P / Tardy ☐ / Homework:	Work G F P / Behavior G F P / Tardy ☐ / Homework:	Work G F P / Behavior G F P / Tardy ☐ / Homework:	Work G F P / Behavior G F P / Tardy ☐ / Homework:
Period 6	Work G F P / Behavior G F P / Tardy ☐ / Homework:	Work G F P / Behavior G F P / Tardy ☐ / Homework:	Work G F P / Behavior G F P / Tardy ☐ / Homework:	Work G F P / Behavior G F P / Tardy ☐ / Homework:	Work G F P / Behavior G F P / Tardy ☐ / Homework:
Period 7	Work G F P / Behavior G F P / Tardy ☐ / Homework:	Work G F P / Behavior G F P / Tardy ☐ / Homework:	Work G F P / Behavior G F P / Tardy ☐ / Homework:	Work G F P / Behavior G F P / Tardy ☐ / Homework:	Work G F P / Behavior G F P / Tardy ☐ / Homework:
Reviewed by:					

See pp. 65–67 for suggestions for use.

Homework Tracking Form

Student Name: _____

Week of: _____

Instructions:
1. The student carries this form to each teacher daily.
2. Each teacher completes and initials the form at the end of class in the box for his or her class.
3. Additional teacher comments may be made on the back of this form.
4. The student reviews this form each day with _____, who initials in the margin at the end of the row for the day.

Monday	Class	Class	Class	Class	Class	Class
	Homework	Homework	Homework	Homework	Homework	Homework
Tuesday	Class	Class	Class	Class	Class	Class
	Homework	Homework	Homework	Homework	Homework	Homework
Wednesday	Class	Class	Class	Class	Class	Class
	Homework	Homework	Homework	Homework	Homework	Homework
Thursday	Class	Class	Class	Class	Class	Class
	Homework	Homework	Homework	Homework	Homework	Homework
Friday	Class	Class	Class	Class	Class	Class
	Homework	Homework	Homework	Homework	Homework	Homework

See pp. 65–67 for suggestions for use.

Daily Tracking Form

Student Name: **Date:**

Period	On Time? Yes / No	Behavior Excellent → Poor 5 4 3 2 1	Prepared? Yes / No	Assignment(s) Completed? Yes / No	Homework Assigned? Yes / No	Teacher's Signature/Initials
1	☐ ☐	5 ☐ 4 ☐ 3 ☐ 2 ☐ 1 ☐	☐ ☐	☐ ☐	☐ ☐	
2	☐ ☐	5 ☐ 4 ☐ 3 ☐ 2 ☐ 1 ☐	☐ ☐	☐ ☐	☐ ☐	
3	☐ ☐	5 ☐ 4 ☐ 3 ☐ 2 ☐ 1 ☐	☐ ☐	☐ ☐	☐ ☐	
4	☐ ☐	5 ☐ 4 ☐ 3 ☐ 2 ☐ 1 ☐	☐ ☐	☐ ☐	☐ ☐	
5	☐ ☐	5 ☐ 4 ☐ 3 ☐ 2 ☐ 1 ☐	☐ ☐	☐ ☐	☐ ☐	
6	☐ ☐	5 ☐ 4 ☐ 3 ☐ 2 ☐ 1 ☐	☐ ☐	☐ ☐	☐ ☐	
7	☐ ☐	5 ☐ 4 ☐ 3 ☐ 2 ☐ 1 ☐	☐ ☐	☐ ☐	☐ ☐	

Homework List (continued on back): _____

_____

_____

_____

_____

Tracking Form Reviewed by:

_____

(Signature)

See pp. 65–67 for suggestions for use.   © 2009 Jenson, Rhode & Reavis

Tough Kid Tool Box

FOR GRADES

3 - 6

Student Tracking Form

Name: Class: Week of:

Day	On Time to Class? Yes No	Had Materials? Yes No	Handed in Assignment(s)? Yes No	Homework Assigned?* Yes No	Appropriate Behavior? Yes No	Teacher's Signature/Initials
Monday	❏ ❏	❏ ❏	❏ ❏	❏ ❏	❏ ❏	
Tuesday	❏ ❏	❏ ❏	❏ ❏	❏ ❏	❏ ❏	
Wednesday	❏ ❏	❏ ❏	❏ ❏	❏ ❏	❏ ❏	
Thursday	❏ ❏	❏ ❏	❏ ❏	❏ ❏	❏ ❏	
Friday	❏ ❏	❏ ❏	❏ ❏	❏ ❏	❏ ❏	

* The student is to list assigned homework on the back of this form.

Tracking Form Reviewed by:

_____

Student Tracking Form

Name: Class: Week of:

Day	On Time to Class? Yes No	Had Materials? Yes No	Handed in Assignment(s)? Yes No	Homework Assigned?* Yes No	Appropriate Behavior? Yes No	Teacher's Signature/Initials
Monday	❏ ❏	❏ ❏	❏ ❏	❏ ❏	❏ ❏	
Tuesday	❏ ❏	❏ ❏	❏ ❏	❏ ❏	❏ ❏	
Wednesday	❏ ❏	❏ ❏	❏ ❏	❏ ❏	❏ ❏	
Thursday	❏ ❏	❏ ❏	❏ ❏	❏ ❏	❏ ❏	
Friday	❏ ❏	❏ ❏	❏ ❏	❏ ❏	❏ ❏	

* The student is to list assigned homework on the back of this form.

Tracking Form Reviewed by:

_____

Tough Kid Tool Box

FOR GRADES
6-12

Behavior Tracking Form

Student Name:

Week of:

Instructions:
1. The student carries this form to each teacher daily.
2. Each teacher completes the rating and initials the form in the appropriate box at the end of class.
3. Additional teacher comments may be made on the back of this form.
4. The student reviews this form each day with _____, who initials the bottom row of this form.

Target Behavior (TB) 1: _____

Target Behavior (TB) 2: _____

Target Behavior (TB) 3: _____

Ratings:
G = Good
F = Fair
P = Poor

	Monday	Tuesday	Wednesday	Thursday	Friday
Period 1	TB 1: G F P TB 2: G F P TB 3: G F P	TB 1: G F P TB 2: G F P TB 3: G F P	TB 1: G F P TB 2: G F P TB 3: G F P	TB 1: G F P TB 2: G F P TB 3: G F P	TB 1: G F P TB 2: G F P TB 3: G F P
Period 2	TB 1: G F P TB 2: G F P TB 3: G F P	TB 1: G F P TB 2: G F P TB 3: G F P	TB 1: G F P TB 2: G F P TB 3: G F P	TB 1: G F P TB 2: G F P TB 3: G F P	TB 1: G F P TB 2: G F P TB 3: G F P
Period 3	TB 1: G F P TB 2: G F P TB 3: G F P	TB 1: G F P TB 2: G F P TB 3: G F P	TB 1: G F P TB 2: G F P TB 3: G F P	TB 1: G F P TB 2: G F P TB 3: G F P	TB 1: G F P TB 2: G F P TB 3: G F P
Period 4	TB 1: G F P TB 2: G F P TB 3: G F P	TB 1: G F P TB 2: G F P TB 3: G F P	TB 1: G F P TB 2: G F P TB 3: G F P	TB 1: G F P TB 2: G F P TB 3: G F P	TB 1: G F P TB 2: G F P TB 3: G F P
Period 5	TB 1: G F P TB 2: G F P TB 3: G F P	TB 1: G F P TB 2: G F P TB 3: G F P	TB 1: G F P TB 2: G F P TB 3: G F P	TB 1: G F P TB 2: G F P TB 3: G F P	TB 1: G F P TB 2: G F P TB 3: G F P
Period 6	TB 1: G F P TB 2: G F P TB 3: G F P	TB 1: G F P TB 2: G F P TB 3: G F P	TB 1: G F P TB 2: G F P TB 3: G F P	TB 1: G F P TB 2: G F P TB 3: G F P	TB 1: G F P TB 2: G F P TB 3: G F P
Period 7	TB 1: G F P TB 2: G F P TB 3: G F P	TB 1: G F P TB 2: G F P TB 3: G F P	TB 1: G F P TB 2: G F P TB 3: G F P	TB 1: G F P TB 2: G F P TB 3: G F P	TB 1: G F P TB 2: G F P TB 3: G F P
Reviewed by:					

See pp. 65–67 for suggestions for use.

Tough Kid Tool Box

FOR GRADES **2-6**

Behavior Tracking Form

Student Name: _____

Week of: _____

Instructions:
1. The student carries this form to each teacher daily.
2. The teacher in each selected setting completes the rating and initials the form at the end of tracking period in the appropriate box.
3. Additional teacher comments may be made on the back of this form.
4. The student reviews this form each day with _____, who initials the bottom row of this form.

Target Behavior (TB) 1: _____

Target Behavior (TB) 2: _____

Target Behavior (TB) 3: _____

Ratings:
1 = Poor
2 = Fair
3 = Average
4 = Very Good
5 = Outstanding

Setting	Monday	Tuesday	Wednesday	Thursday	Friday
Setting	TB 1: 1 2 3 4 5 TB 2: 1 2 3 4 5 TB 3: 1 2 3 4 5	TB 1: 1 2 3 4 5 TB 2: 1 2 3 4 5 TB 3: 1 2 3 4 5	TB 1: 1 2 3 4 5 TB 2: 1 2 3 4 5 TB 3: 1 2 3 4 5	TB 1: 1 2 3 4 5 TB 2: 1 2 3 4 5 TB 3: 1 2 3 4 5	TB 1: 1 2 3 4 5 TB 2: 1 2 3 4 5 TB 3: 1 2 3 4 5
Setting	TB 1: 1 2 3 4 5 TB 2: 1 2 3 4 5 TB 3: 1 2 3 4 5	TB 1: 1 2 3 4 5 TB 2: 1 2 3 4 5 TB 3: 1 2 3 4 5	TB 1: 1 2 3 4 5 TB 2: 1 2 3 4 5 TB 3: 1 2 3 4 5	TB 1: 1 2 3 4 5 TB 2: 1 2 3 4 5 TB 3: 1 2 3 4 5	TB 1: 1 2 3 4 5 TB 2: 1 2 3 4 5 TB 3: 1 2 3 4 5
Setting	TB 1: 1 2 3 4 5 TB 2: 1 2 3 4 5 TB 3: 1 2 3 4 5	TB 1: 1 2 3 4 5 TB 2: 1 2 3 4 5 TB 3: 1 2 3 4 5	TB 1: 1 2 3 4 5 TB 2: 1 2 3 4 5 TB 3: 1 2 3 4 5	TB 1: 1 2 3 4 5 TB 2: 1 2 3 4 5 TB 3: 1 2 3 4 5	TB 1: 1 2 3 4 5 TB 2: 1 2 3 4 5 TB 3: 1 2 3 4 5
Setting	TB 1: 1 2 3 4 5 TB 2: 1 2 3 4 5 TB 3: 1 2 3 4 5	TB 1: 1 2 3 4 5 TB 2: 1 2 3 4 5 TB 3: 1 2 3 4 5	TB 1: 1 2 3 4 5 TB 2: 1 2 3 4 5 TB 3: 1 2 3 4 5	TB 1: 1 2 3 4 5 TB 2: 1 2 3 4 5 TB 3: 1 2 3 4 5	TB 1: 1 2 3 4 5 TB 2: 1 2 3 4 5 TB 3: 1 2 3 4 5
Setting	TB 1: 1 2 3 4 5 TB 2: 1 2 3 4 5 TB 3: 1 2 3 4 5	TB 1: 1 2 3 4 5 TB 2: 1 2 3 4 5 TB 3: 1 2 3 4 5	TB 1: 1 2 3 4 5 TB 2: 1 2 3 4 5 TB 3: 1 2 3 4 5	TB 1: 1 2 3 4 5 TB 2: 1 2 3 4 5 TB 3: 1 2 3 4 5	TB 1: 1 2 3 4 5 TB 2: 1 2 3 4 5 TB 3: 1 2 3 4 5
Setting	TB 1: 1 2 3 4 5 TB 2: 1 2 3 4 5 TB 3: 1 2 3 4 5	TB 1: 1 2 3 4 5 TB 2: 1 2 3 4 5 TB 3: 1 2 3 4 5	TB 1: 1 2 3 4 5 TB 2: 1 2 3 4 5 TB 3: 1 2 3 4 5	TB 1: 1 2 3 4 5 TB 2: 1 2 3 4 5 TB 3: 1 2 3 4 5	TB 1: 1 2 3 4 5 TB 2: 1 2 3 4 5 TB 3: 1 2 3 4 5
Setting	TB 1: 1 2 3 4 5 TB 2: 1 2 3 4 5 TB 3: 1 2 3 4 5	TB 1: 1 2 3 4 5 TB 2: 1 2 3 4 5 TB 3: 1 2 3 4 5	TB 1: 1 2 3 4 5 TB 2: 1 2 3 4 5 TB 3: 1 2 3 4 5	TB 1: 1 2 3 4 5 TB 2: 1 2 3 4 5 TB 3: 1 2 3 4 5	TB 1: 1 2 3 4 5 TB 2: 1 2 3 4 5 TB 3: 1 2 3 4 5
Reviewed by:					

See pp. 65–67 for suggestions for use.

Unique Reinforcers

def•i•ni•tion

Positive reinforcement involves the contingent presentation of something valued or desired by the student. This "something" the student values (the *reinforcer*) is given immediately **after** the desired behavior occurs and results in an increase in the behavior.

de•scrip•tion

It is an indisputable fact that the behaviors that are supported and recognized are the ones that will increase. The trick is for teachers to positively support and recognize Tough Kids' appropriate behavior in ways that are **meaningful to them.** Once teachers' classroom rules have been established at the beginning of the school year, the major driving force behind their classroom management must be the way they motivate and recognize students.

Tough Kids' teachers must find unique and interesting ways to consistently provide motivation and recognition to these students for exhibiting the behaviors they desire to increase. If adequate motivation and recognition are not in place, no classroom management plan will **ever** be effective. Some unique reinforcer ideas follow.

> *"Behaviors that are supported and recognized are the ones that will increase."*

REINFORCER MENUS

def•i•ni•tion

A reinforcer menu is a list of known reinforcers (or a "list" of pictures cut from magazines or drawn) that the student likes. When selecting a reward, the student need only point to the item of choice. This method is particularly useful with students who have difficulty communicating their needs and wants.

de•scrip•tion

Items listed or depicted on a reinforcer menu should be changed and updated periodically so that they remain novel and desirable to the student. "Wild Card" or "Mystery" items may also be included on the menu to increase anticipation. These items should not be known by the student ahead of time.

Using Reinforcer Menus

The reinforcer menus provided in this section's reproducible tools (Reproducibles 6-1 through 6-5) may be copied or printed from the CD for consumable use or laminated onto poster board for continued use with water-based markers. With either method, changing the reinforcers regularly is a simple task.

SPINNERS

def•i•ni•tion

A game-type Spinner like the one shown in Figure 6-1 may be used to reinforce numerous behaviors. The Spinner is divided into five or more sections of various sizes. Each section of the Spinner represents a different positive reinforcer. Being first in line to lunch, a new pencil, ten minutes of free time with a friend, and an edible treat would be appropriate reinforcers for elementary students. Secondary students enjoy earning coupons exchangeable for gas for their cars, food from a fast food restaurant, a parking space in front of the school for a day, or hair styling services.

de•scrip•tion

Positive reinforcement represented on the Spinner should be planned and selected with the student. Positive reinforcers of "higher" value are given smaller sections of the Spinner. When used in conjunction with the Chart Moves system (following), the student earns a spin on the Spinner when he reaches one of the colored reward dots. Like the reinforcer menu, items represented on the Spinner must be changed often enough to keep student interest high.

Using Spinners

Choose the Spinner design you wish to use from those provided in this section's reproducible tools (Reproducibles 6-6a and 6-6b). Laminate it onto poster board, cut on the dotted line to remove the arrow, and cut out the arrow. Fasten the arrow to the Spinner's center with a small metal brad.

Figure 6-1: Spinner Example

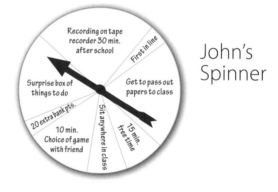

CHART MOVES

def•i•ni•tion

Chart Moves is a technique utilizing dot-to-dot pictures that are posted so that students can track their own progress. The chart determines when rewards will be delivered (see Figure 6-2).

de•scrip•tion

With Chart Moves (Reproducibles 6-8a-f), each time reinforcement is earned, the student is allowed to connect another dot on the chart. The prespecified reward is earned each time a special reward dot is reached. The reward dots are colored or circled to indicate when the student will receive the reward. Additionally, the first or last chart move earned each day may be dated so that a student's daily progress is automatically recorded as the chart is used.

Maximizing the Effectiveness of Chart Moves

The distance (or number of chart moves) between the special reward dots should vary depending on the frequency with which you believe the student's behavior must be rewarded. A student should be required to make fewer chart moves initially to reach the reward dot when she is first learning a new behavior. Reward dots should be spaced further apart (requiring more chart moves) as a student's behavior improves.

Chart Moves Variations

1 **Chart Moves may be combined with the use of invisible-ink pens, available at** most office supply stores or www.crayola.com. With this strategy, the reward dots are not circled or colored on the chart, but rather are marked with an invisible-ink pen. Each time the student earns a chart move, he touches the next dot with the developer pen, which turns the dot a dark color if it has been designated as a reward dot by the invisible-ink pen. Thus, reinforcement is unpredictable and will usually result in high performance rates.

2 **You can make a dot-to-dot chart that is an actual picture of what the student wishes to earn.** For example, a drawing of an ice cream cone, an action figure, or a squirt gun might be used as the outline for the chart. Similarly, the student might earn a puzzle piece each time she lands on a reward dot. When completed, the puzzle forms a picture of the earned item, and the student receives the item when the puzzle is complete.

3 **Instead of connecting dots on the chart, the student can earn the privilege of coloring in blocks of a graphed reinforcement tower** (see Figure 6-3). When the student reaches a predetermined level of the tower, certain pre-specified positive reinforcement is delivered.

Figure 6-2: Chart Moves Examples

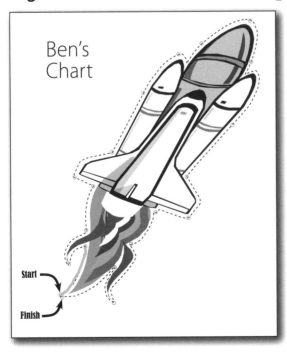

Ben's Chart

Start
Finish

Start
Finish

Mary's Chart

Figure 6-3

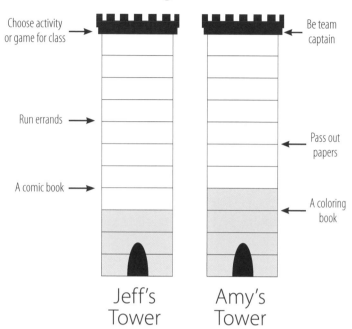

Choose activity or game for class →

Run errands →

A comic book →

← Be team captain

← Pass out papers

← A coloring book

Jeff's Tower   Amy's Tower

LOTTERY/RAFFLE TICKETS

 def•i•ni•tion

Lottery or raffle tickets are small rectangles of paper that may carry a positive message and a place for recipients to write their names. The tickets are given to students to recognize specifically targeted appropriate behavior you wish to increase.

de•scrip•tion

Students write their names on earned tickets and deposit them in a designated container in the classroom. Depending on how frequently you need to reinforce your class, drawings for small prizes may be held once or twice each day as well as weekly or monthly. The more reinforcement the class requires, the more frequently drawings should be held and the more prizes awarded each time.

Steps for Implementing Lottery/Raffle Tickets

STEP 1 Select the specific academic and/or social behavior(s) you wish to improve.

STEP 2 Select the tickets you wish to use from those provided in this section's reproducible tools (Reproducibles 6-9a–e).

STEP 3 Determine how often initial drawings must be held for the students to be motivated to work for the tickets.

STEP 4 Explain the program to the students. Tell them the behaviors that will result in their earning the tickets. Give examples of the desired behaviors; role-play if necessary to make certain the students understand the expectations.

STEP 5 Implement the program. Give tickets generously for the targeted behaviors.

STEP 6 When giving out each ticket, specifically describe and praise the behavior for which the ticket is being given.

STEP 7 Be certain to award tickets to students who have not exhibited the targeted behaviors previously but are exhibiting them now.

STEP 8 Be certain to also award tickets to students who **have** exhibited the target behaviors in the past and **continue** to exhibit them. Otherwise, the students may get the idea that the only way they will receive reinforcement is if they first fail to behave appropriately.

STEP 9 Within two weeks of implementing a daily raffle program, or four weeks of implementing a weekly one, evaluate the effectiveness of the program. Make adjustments as necessary in the target behaviors, the prizes that are awarded in the drawings, the frequency of the drawings, and the number of tickets available for students to earn each day.

Maximizing the Effectiveness of Lottery/Raffle Tickets

1 **Build in a "cost" or "fine" system so that Tough Kids who have just recently exhibited inappropriate behavior are not rewarded by the system.** To prevent this type of occurrence, a rule may be adopted specifying that any student will be disqualified from collecting a prize when her name is drawn in that particular drawing if her inappropriate behavior has necessitated being sent to the office or required a phone call home to parents

"Make adjustments as necessary in the target behaviors."

(or earned another classroom penalty for severe behavior problems) during that day (for a daily drawing) or during the week before a weekly or monthly drawing.

2 **Keep a list of students who are disqualified, in case their names are drawn in the raffle.** If a disqualified student's name is drawn, it is not necessary, nor desirable, to announce the name. Merely state that the name of someone who has been disqualified has been drawn and that another name will be selected. This procedure maximizes the "fine" system because all the students who have been disqualified for the drawing will think they may have collected a prize had they not been disqualified.

THE YES/NO PROGRAM

 def•i•ni•tion

The Yes/No program is a simple individual or group contingency program for reinforcing academic or social behavior.

 **de•scrip•tion**

For younger students or students with severe disabilities, copy the set of tickets (Reproducible 6-11) with a smiley face to denote "Yes" and a frowny face to denote "No." For older or less disabled students, select the tickets with the "Yes" and "No" words (Reproducible 6-10).

Steps for Implementing the Yes/No Program

STEP 1 Select a specific target behavior to increase. Behaviors such as increasing compliance with teacher requests, raising one's hand to talk, staying in one's seat, and positive comments to others are examples of behaviors to target for use with this program.

STEP 2 Select the reinforcers that can be earned by the students participating in the program.

STEP 3 Select the Yes/No tickets that are appropriate for the students who will be using them and make several copies of the page.

STEP 4 Before beginning the program, explain it in detail to the students participating. Make certain they understand the behaviors that will earn them a "Yes" ticket and those that will earn them a "No." Role-play examples and non-examples of the behaviors that will earn a "Yes" or "No." Answer any questions the students have about the program.

STEP 5 Implement the program. When a student engages in the target behaviors, mark the "Yes" or "smiley" designation on a ticket, write the student's name on it, and deposit it in a predetermined container. If a student does not exhibit the target behaviors when it is appropriate to do so, mark the "No" or "frowny" designation on the ticket, write the student's name on it, and deposit it in the container.

For example, if the target behavior is "following teacher directions immediately" (within 5–10 seconds) and the student complies right away, a "Yes" is marked on a ticket, the student's name written on it, and the ticket deposited in the container. If the student does not comply right away, a "No" is marked, the student's name written on the ticket, and the ticket deposited in the container. Give out at least three "Yes" tickets for every "No" ticket.

STEP 6 Give the student specific feedback for each "Yes" or "No" earned. For example, if the target behavior is "compliance" and the student complies, you might say, "Rocky, you followed my directions right away. You just earned a 'Yes' ticket." If the student does not comply, you might say, "Rocky, that's not following my directions. You just earned a 'No' ticket."

STEP 7 At the end of the designated time period (e.g., a specific class session such as reading or math, or at the end of the school day for a daily drawing), hold the Yes/No drawing. Select several tickets from the container and pass out rewards or privileges for those drawn with a "Yes" marked on them. Tickets selected that are marked "No" result in no reinforcement.

TECHNIQUE TIP

To maximize the effectiveness of the Yes/No program and to avoid public embarrassment of students who earned "No" tickets, when a ticket is selected with a "No" on it, simply say, "I'm sorry, but I've just drawn a ticket with a 'No' on it. That person forfeits the prize." By handling the "No"s in this manner, all students who have earned "No"s will think it might be their ticket. ~

STEP 8 Keep track of whether the target behavior is actually increasing. If it is not, consider changing the reinforcers that can be earned or increasing the frequency of drawings. Also, make certain that the target behavior is defined specifically enough so that the students understand exactly what behaviors will earn a "Yes." Make certain that tickets are awarded consistently, based on the defined target behaviors.

STEP 9 Once the target behavior is occurring regularly at acceptable levels, gradually fade the use of the program. For example, instead of awarding a "Yes" every time a student exhibits the target behaviors, give one after an average of every second time, every third time, and so on. Continue to award a "No" for each instance when the target behavior is not demonstrated when it should be.

POINT SYSTEMS

 def•i•ni•tion

Points are part of a reinforcement system in which target behaviors are reinforced as soon as possible after their occurrence by the teacher awarding points to the student. The teacher awards the points while praising the student for the specific appropriate behavior he or she just exhibited.

 de•scrip•tion

When points are awarded, they are recorded by the teacher (or by the student at your direction) on a point card (provided in this section's reproducible tools, Reproducibles 6-12a and b) or other record-keeping system. Points can later be exchanged for reinforcing objects or activities.

Steps for Implementing Point Systems

STEP 1 Determine the behaviors to be increased or decreased through the use of a point system. These may include academic behaviors (e.g., increasing reading or math fact rates), social behaviors (e.g., sharing, responding calmly to teasing), and/or classroom survival skills (e.g., staying in one's seat, raising one's hand to talk).

STEP 2 Determine the items, activities, or privileges for which points can be exchanged. Effective reinforcers can be identified by asking the students what they would like to earn, observing how the students spend their free time, using reinforcer checklists, or allowing the students to **sample** potential reinforcers without first having to earn them in order to see what they select.

STEP 3 Decide on the number of points that can be earned for exhibiting the target behaviors. Also, determine the time frame in which they may be earned. For example, you may decide that up to five points can be earned for raising hands and waiting to be called on during the daily 30-minute reading group.

STEP 4 Determine the reinforcer "costs" in terms of points. Classroom demand for reinforcers should ultimately determine their cost. Although there are no hard and fast rules, one idea is to initially equate the actual cost of an item with a certain number of points. Five points for each cent of cost (e.g., a 25¢ toy would cost 125 points) is reasonable for students who can earn an average of 50 points per day.

TECHNIQUE TIP

Typically, a point system should offer two types of reinforcers—small and large. Small items should be priced so a typical student can earn something each day. Larger reinforcers should require more points so students can earn them only by saving points over a period of time. Publicly post reinforcer costs in the classroom to serve as a reminder and as a motivator to the students. ~

STEP 5 A "classroom bank" or some other type of record-keeping system will be required to keep track of points earned and spent. A "bank" may consist of a large laminated list of students' names on which you can write with a water-based marker and erase as point totals change for each student (see Reproducible 6-13).

TECHNIQUE TIP

Publicly posting the bank amounts provides feedback to the students about how well they are doing and fosters competition to earn more points for appropriate behavior. ~

STEP 6 Decide on a system for delivering points to students. Points should be dispensed quickly and unobtrusively immediately after the appropriate behavior for which they are earned.

TECHNIQUE TIP

As points are earned, they may be recorded on individual point cards on students' desks or carried on a teacher clipboard. ~

STEP 7 Explain procedures to the students ahead of time.

TECHNIQUE TIP

The rules for earning points and the specific behaviors for which points can be earned should be posted in the classroom, explained to the students, and clearly understood by them ahead of time. This may require modeling, role-playing and demonstration of examples and non-examples of the use of the procedure by the teacher. ~

STEP 8 When you use a point system, social reinforcement or praise must always accompany the dispensing of points. The social reinforcement should specifically describe the behavior that the student exhibited that resulted in the earning of points. Both the points and the praise statement should be delivered quickly, with the teacher moving on to the next student or back to the instructional task at hand so as to cause as little disruption as possible.

"Publicly post reinforcer costs in the classroom to serve as a motivator to the students."

STEP 9 When the students are first learning the target behaviors, the points should be delivered on a continuous basis, or after each occurrence of the behaviors. Once the behaviors have been acquired, the schedule of delivery for points must gradually shift from continuous to intermittent (e.g., awarding of points to every fourth occurrence, on average, of the target behaviors). High rates of praise for appropriate behavior should be maintained, even though points awarded for appropriate behaviors will decrease.

STEP 10 Make adjustments as necessary. Change reinforcer point "prices" as demand dictates and to avoid problems such as point hoarding. Likewise, you may need to change the backup reinforcers regularly so that there is always something available that every student would like to earn. Schedules of delivery of points from continuous to intermittent will also require change to remain effective.

Point System Variations

1 Permit peers to share reinforcers they have earned with each other. Allowing peers to share each other's earned reinforcers may help improve the students' motivation to earn those reinforcers themselves.

2 Use a peer management system. Enlisting students to help record points earned, dispense reinforcers, and withdraw points can improve the students' motivation to earn reinforcers. The privilege of helping to operate the point system can also be used as a reinforcer that students may earn.

3 Combine the point system with a group contingency. With a group contingency, the entire group's performance determines whether each individual in that group will earn points.

4 Combine lottery or raffle tickets with the use of a point system. Earned points may be used to "purchase" lottery or raffle tickets for a classroom drawing. The more points a student has earned for appropriate behavior, the more lottery or raffle tickets she will be able to buy.

Troubleshooting Point Systems

1 Failure to specifically define the target behaviors that earn points may result in inconsistent implementation of the point system and confusion for students. You and the students must all have a **clear** understanding ahead of time of the behaviors that will result in the awarding of points.

2 Pricing reinforcers too low will enable the students to earn many reinforcers in a short period of time, reducing their motivation to perform appropriately over a longer period of time. Likewise, pricing reinforcers too high can result in students giving up, believing that it is too difficult to earn the reinforcers.

3 Sometimes students will attempt to "counterfeit" points on their point cards. Select a system of awarding points that will prevent student counterfeiting. For example, award points on the students' cards with an unusual color of pen.

4 Sometimes there may not be enough variety in the reinforcers being offered. Periodically change and update the items, activities, or privileges for which points can be exchanged. Every participating student must find a reinforcer that is appealing and available in order for the system to be effective.

5 Students who are permitted to accumulate large hoards of points may believe that they can "coast" for a period of time and not work or behave appropriately until they run out of points. Hoarding may also result in a student's being able to purchase a large number of prized reinforcers in one day, thus making them unavailable for the other students. Hoarding may be reduced by specifying expiration dates for the spending of points or by having a classroom store sale or auction.

Rules for an auction would include: (1) all point savings are dropped to zero the day after the auction, (2) the students bid against each other for the available items, and (3) the students cannot lend each other points for the auction.

6 A decrease in appropriate student behaviors after fading the point system may be due to too large of a jump in the reinforcement schedule. For example, you may have switched from giving points on a continuous schedule for hand raising to giving points on an intermittent schedule for an average of every tenth hand raise. If this is the case, switch back to a very brief period of continuous reinforcement and then try a smaller ratio, such as an average of every two or three hand raises.

7 A decrease in appropriate student behaviors after fading the point system could also occur because you neglected to pair social reinforcement with the delivery of each point. In this case, when the points are faded, nothing naturally reinforcing is in place to maintain the newly acquired behaviors. To solve this problem, return to the previous point level and begin the delivery of points combined with social reinforcement before attempting to fade the points again. Be sure to retain the social reinforcement even after the use of points is reduced.

8 Behavior deterioration may also be due to too great of a delay in awarding points after appropriate behavior has occurred or too great of a delay in exchanging points for reinforcers. Points should be awarded **immediately** after the appropriate behaviors, and point exchange opportunities may have to be increased initially to be effective.

⚠ CAUTION

All students have civil rights to water, food, clothing, and use of the bathroom. These cannot be used as reinforcement to earn with points.

Tough Kid Tool Box

Unique Reinforcers
Reproducible Tools

Both Spanish and English
versions of all
REPRODUCIBLE
TOOLS
appear on the CD.

Reinforcer Menu

1

2

3

4

5

6

See pp. 75 and 76 for suggestions for use.

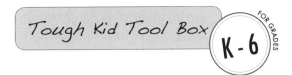

Reinforcer Menu

1

2

3

4

5

6   Wild Card

Tough Kid Tool Box

K-6

FOR GRADES

Elementary Reinforcer Menu
With Key

Student Name _____

Instructions:

Ask the student to write a check (✔) next to at least eight items/activities he or she would most like to earn in class. (Read the list to non-readers and help them mark the items they select.)

_____ 1. Blow bubbles

_____ 2. Ice cream

_____ 3. Coloring/drawing

_____ 4. Gym time

_____ 5. Play with friends

_____ 6. Puzzles

_____ 7. Stickers

_____ 8. Use tape recorder

_____ 9. Cookie

_____ 10. Write on chalkboard

_____ 11. Computer time

_____ 12. Pudding

_____ 13. Video games

_____ 14. Be in a program

_____ 15. Extra recess

_____ 16. Lollipop

_____ 17. Carry messages

_____ 18. Building blocks

_____ 19. Time with a grown-up

_____ 20. Fruit juice

_____ 21. Storytime

_____ 22. Good note home

_____ 23. Soda pop

_____ 24. Popcorn

See pp. 75 and 76 for suggestions for use.

Tough Kid Tool Box

K-6 FOR GRADES

Elementary Reinforcer Menu

Student Name _____

Instructions:

Ask the student to write a check (✔) next to at least eight items/activities he or she would most like to earn in class. (Read the list to non-readers and help them mark the items they select.)

Write available items/activities to the right of each item number.

_____ 1. _____	_____ 13. _____
_____ 2. _____	_____ 14. _____
_____ 3. _____	_____ 15. _____
_____ 4. _____	_____ 16. _____
_____ 5. _____	_____ 17. _____
_____ 6. _____	_____ 18. _____
_____ 7. _____	_____ 19. _____
_____ 8. _____	_____ 20. _____
_____ 9. _____	_____ 21. _____
_____ 10. _____	_____ 22. _____
_____ 11. _____	_____ 23. _____
_____ 12. _____	_____ 24. _____

Tough Kid Tool Box **7-12** FOR GRADES

Secondary Reinforcer Menu With Key

Student Name _____ Class Period _____

Instructions to Student:

Write a check (✔) next to at least eight items/activities you would like to earn in class.

_____	1. Listen to Top 40 music
_____	2. Skip a homework assignment
_____	3. Talk to a friend
_____	4. Soda pop
_____	5. Ticket to a sporting event
_____	6. Watch a movie
_____	7. Pizza
_____	8. Listen to MP3 player
_____	9. Class trip
_____	10. Fast food coupon
_____	11. Snack food
_____	12. School supplies
_____	13. Play a video game
_____	14. Computer time
_____	15. Play basketball or another sport
_____	16. Read
_____	17. Ticket to a school dance
_____	18. Participate in an assembly
_____	19. Class party
_____	20. Drawing

See pp. 75 and 76 for suggestions for use.

Tough Kid Tool Box

FOR GRADES

7-12

Secondary Reinforcer Menu

Student Name _____   Class Period _____

Instructions to Student:

Write a check (✔) next to at least eight items/activities you would like to earn in class.

Teacher: Write available items/activities to the right of each item number.

_____   1. _____

_____   2. _____

_____   3. _____

_____   4. _____

_____   5. _____

_____   6. _____

_____   7. _____

_____   8. _____

_____   9. _____

_____   10. _____

_____   11. _____

_____   12. _____

_____   13. _____

_____   14. _____

_____   15. _____

_____   16. _____

_____   17. _____

_____   18. _____

_____   19. _____

_____   20. _____

See pp. 75 and 76 for suggestions for use.

© 2009 Jenson, Rhode & Reavis

Tough Kid Tool Box

K-12 FOR GRADES

Spinner

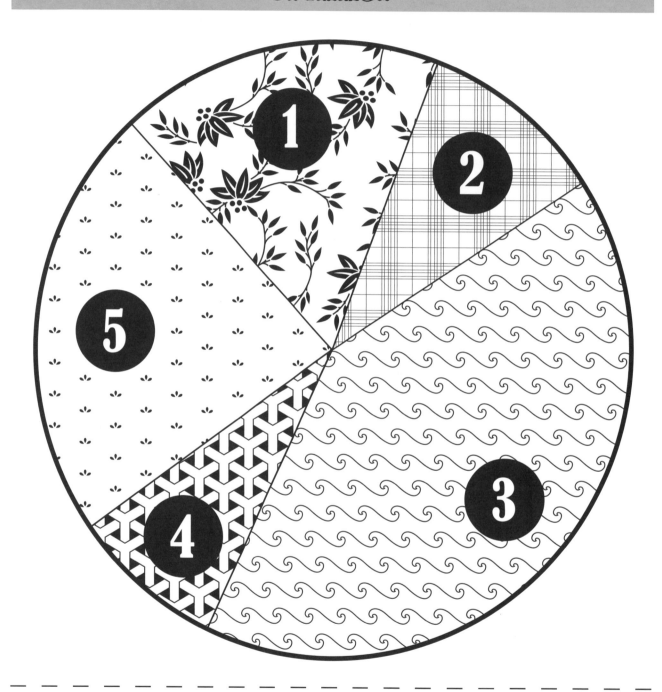

Spinner

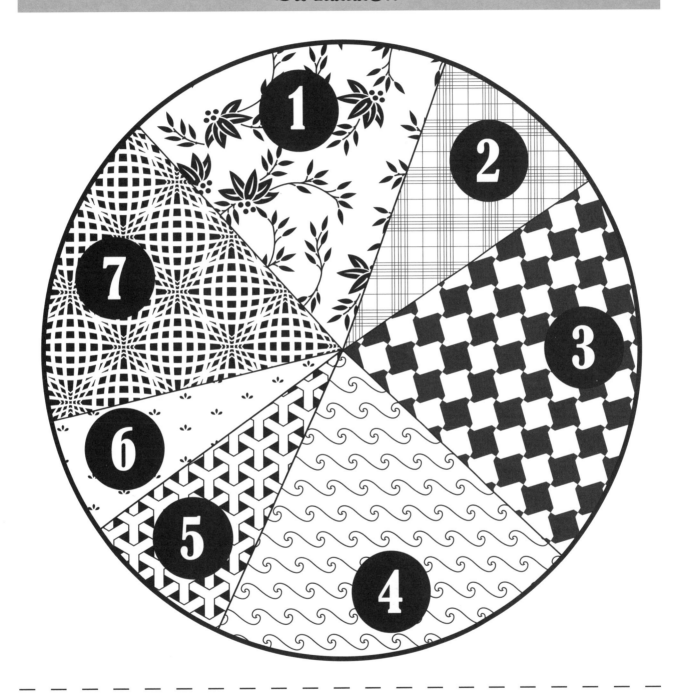

See p. 76 for suggestions for use.

Tough Kid Tool Box

K-6 FOR GRADES

Reinforcement Tower

Name _____

See pp. 76–78 for suggestions for use.

Tough Kid Tool Box — K-6 FOR GRADES

Chart Moves

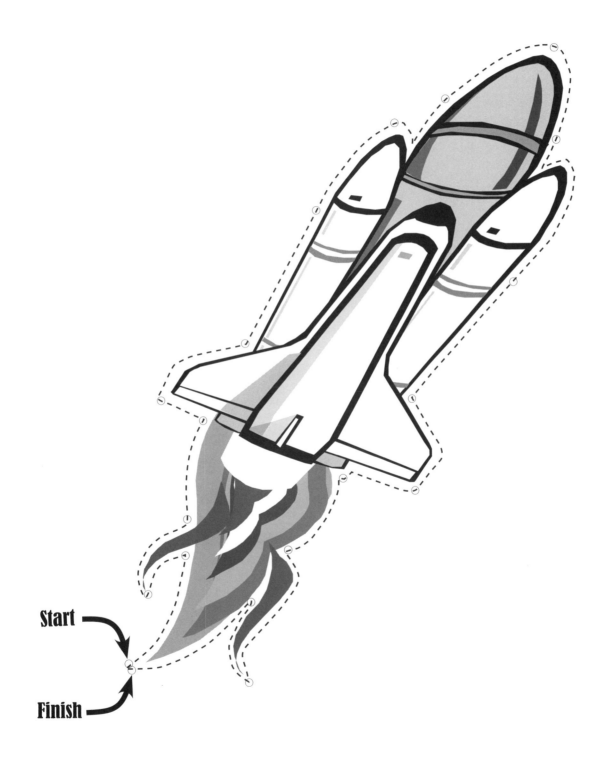

Start

Finish

Name _____

Tough Kid Tool Box

K-6

FOR GRADES

Chart Moves

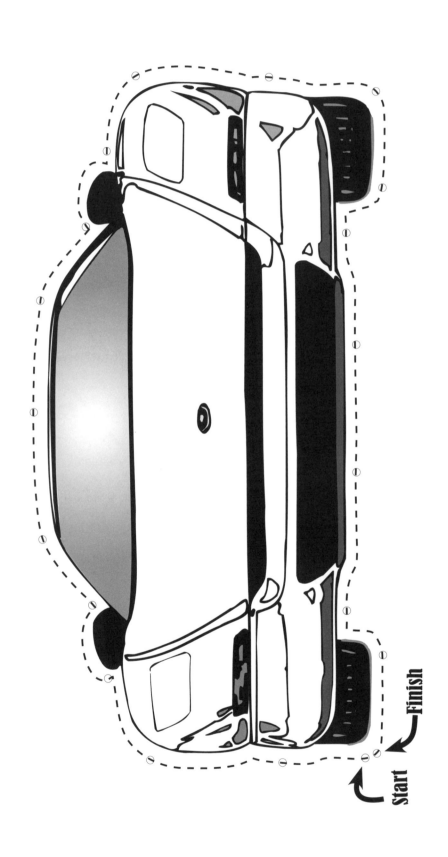

Start

Finish

Name

Chart Moves

Start

Finish

Name _____

© *2009 Jenson, Rhode & Reavis*

Tough Kid Tool Box **K-6** FOR GRADES

Chart Moves

Start

Finish

Name _____

Chart Moves

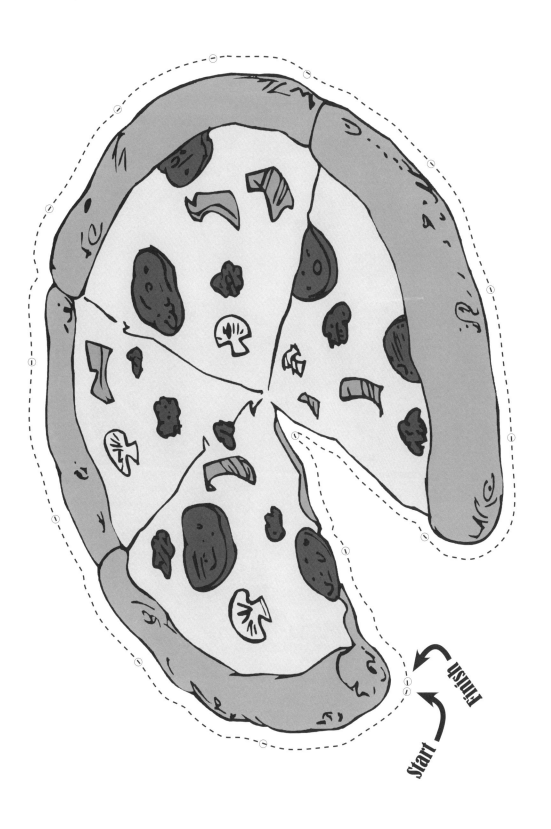

Start

Finish

Name

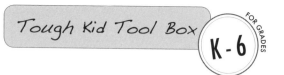

Chart Moves

Name _____

See pp. 76–78 for suggestions for use.

Tough Kid Tool Box

FOR GRADES
K-6

Lottery/Raffle Tickets

Soaring with the Eagles

Awarded to _____

for Exceptional Performance!

Soaring with the Eagles

Awarded to _____

for Exceptional Performance!

Soaring with the Eagles

Awarded to _____

for Exceptional Performance!

Soaring with the Eagles

Awarded to _____

for Exceptional Performance!

Soaring with the Eagles

Awarded to _____

for Exceptional Performance!

Soaring with the Eagles

Awarded to _____

for Exceptional Performance!

Soaring with the Eagles

Awarded to _____

for Exceptional Performance!

Soaring with the Eagles

Awarded to _____

for Exceptional Performance!

Soaring with the Eagles

Awarded to _____

for Exceptional Performance!

Soaring with the Eagles

Awarded to _____

for Exceptional Performance!

Soaring with the Eagles

Awarded to _____

for Exceptional Performance!

Soaring with the Eagles

Awarded to _____

for Exceptional Performance!

See pp. 78 and 79 for suggestions for use.

Tough Kid Tool Box

FOR GRADES K-6

Lottery/Raffle Tickets

Pot O' Gold
Chance Card
Awarded to:

Pot O' Gold
Chance Card
Awarded to:

Pot O' Gold
Chance Card
Awarded to:

Pot O' Gold
Chance Card
Awarded to:

Pot O' Gold
Chance Card
Awarded to:

Pot O' Gold
Chance Card
Awarded to:

Pot O' Gold
Chance Card
Awarded to:

Pot O' Gold
Chance Card
Awarded to:

Pot O' Gold
Chance Card
Awarded to:

Pot O' Gold
Chance Card
Awarded to:

Pot O' Gold
Chance Card
Awarded to:

Pot O' Gold
Chance Card
Awarded to:

See pp. 78 and 79 for suggestions for use.

Tough Kid Tool Box

K-6 FOR GRADES

Lottery/Raffle Tickets

I was caught doing a SUPER JOB!

Awarded to:
_____

I was caught doing a SUPER JOB!

Awarded to:
_____

I was caught doing a SUPER JOB!

Awarded to:
_____

I was caught doing a SUPER JOB!

Awarded to:
_____

I was caught doing a SUPER JOB!

Awarded to:
_____

I was caught doing a SUPER JOB!

Awarded to:
_____

I was caught doing a SUPER JOB!

Awarded to:
_____

I was caught doing a SUPER JOB!

Awarded to:
_____

I was caught doing a SUPER JOB!

Awarded to:
_____

I was caught doing a SUPER JOB!

Awarded to:
_____

I was caught doing a SUPER JOB!

Awarded to:
_____

I was caught doing a SUPER JOB!

Awarded to:
_____

See pp. 78 and 79 for suggestions for use.

Tough Kid Tool Box

K-6

FOR GRADES

Lottery/Raffle Tickets

No Use Lion— I've Been Tryin'!

Awarded to:

See pp. 78 and 79 for suggestions for use.

Tough Kid Tool Box

FOR GRADES **K-6**

Lottery/Raffle Tickets

Classroom Pride
Ticket for Outstanding
Performance

Awarded to: _____

Classroom Pride
Ticket for Outstanding
Performance

Awarded to: _____

Classroom Pride
Ticket for Outstanding
Performance

Awarded to: _____

Classroom Pride
Ticket for Outstanding
Performance

Awarded to: _____

Classroom Pride
Ticket for Outstanding
Performance

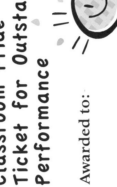

Awarded to: _____

Classroom Pride
Ticket for Outstanding
Performance

Awarded to: _____

Classroom Pride
Ticket for Outstanding
Performance

Awarded to: _____

Classroom Pride
Ticket for Outstanding
Performance

Awarded to: _____

Classroom Pride
Ticket for Outstanding
Performance

Awarded to: _____

Classroom Pride
Ticket for Outstanding
Performance

Awarded to: _____

Classroom Pride
Ticket for Outstanding
Performance

Awarded to: _____

Classroom Pride
Ticket for Outstanding
Performance

Awarded to: _____

See pp. 78 and 79 for suggestions for use.

Tough Kid Tool Box

FOR GRADES 4 - 6

YES/NO Tickets

YES NO	YES NO	YES NO	YES NO
Name _____	Name _____	Name _____	Name _____
YES NO	YES NO	YES NO	YES NO
Name _____	Name _____	Name _____	Name _____
YES NO	YES NO	YES NO	YES NO
Name _____	Name _____	Name _____	Name _____
YES NO	YES NO	YES NO	YES NO
Name _____	Name _____	Name _____	Name _____

See pp. 79–81 for suggestions for use.

Tough Kid Tool Box

K-3 FOR GRADES

Smiley/Frowny Tickets

☺ ☹	☺ ☹	☺ ☹	☺ ☹
Name _____	**Name** _____	**Name** _____	**Name** _____
☺ ☹	☺ ☹	☺ ☹	☺ ☹
Name _____	**Name** _____	**Name** _____	**Name** _____
☺ ☹	☺ ☹	☺ ☹	☺ ☹
Name _____	**Name** _____	**Name** _____	**Name** _____
☺ ☹	☺ ☹	☺ ☹	☺ ☹
Name _____	**Name** _____	**Name** _____	**Name** _____

See pp. 79–81 for suggestions for use.

Point Cards

	1	2	3	4	5	6	7	8	9	10
1										
2										
3										
4										
5										
6										
7										
8										
9										
10										

Name _____

	1	2	3	4	5	6	7	8	9	10
1										
2										
3										
4										
5										
6										
7										
8										
9										
10										

Name _____

	1	2	3	4	5	6	7	8	9	10
1										
2										
3										
4										
5										
6										
7										
8										
9										
10										

Name _____

	1	2	3	4	5	6	7	8	9	10
1										
2										
3										
4										
5										
6										
7										
8										
9										
10										

Name _____

See pp. 81–84 for suggestions for use.

Point Cards

	1	2	3	4	5	6	7	8	9	10
1										
2										
3										
4										
5										
6										
7										
8										
9										
10										

Name _____

	1	2	3	4	5	6	7	8	9	10
1										
2										
3										
4										
5										
6										
7										
8										
9										
10										

Name _____

	1	2	3	4	5	6	7	8	9	10
1										
2										
3										
4										
5										
6										
7										
8										
9										
10										

Name _____

	1	2	3	4	5	6	7	8	9	10
1										
2										
3										
4										
5										
6										
7										
8										
9										
10										

Name _____

See pp. 81–84 for suggestions for use.

Tough Kid Tool Box

K-6 FOR GRADES

Classroom Bank Points

Name	Mon	Tue	Wed	Thur	Fri	Total

See pp. 81–84 for suggestions for use.

General Interventions

This section provides a variety of interventions with detailed instructions for their use. Ready-to-use materials to accompany each may be found in this section's reproducible tools.

THE WHAT IF? CHART

def•i•ni•tion

The What If? Chart is a chart that summarizes your classroom management plan in terms of preplanned positive consequences, reductive consequences, and consequences for very serious behavior problems.

de•scrip•tion

All too often, only negative reductive consequences are specified in a classroom management plan. But a What If? Chart will also list, on the left-hand side, positive consequences that students will receive if they follow the classroom rules. Including positive consequences offers a well-balanced approach to classroom consequences (see Chapter 3 of *The Tough Kid Book* for examples of preplanned reductive consequences, positive consequences, and serious behavior clauses).

A What If? Chart lists a preplanned hierarchy of reductive consequences on the right-hand side, along with how much or how long each consequence will be used. The reductive consequences increase in severity as they go down the hierarchy on the chart (see Reproducible 7-1).

> *"Most well-designed sets of classroom rules will evolve and be refined over time."*

The reductive consequences should be used **only** if: (1) the pre-established classroom rules are broken or (2) a student does not comply with your request. If a misbehavior occurs that is not addressed in the classroom rules, the classroom rules should be re-examined. Most well-designed sets of classroom rules will evolve and be refined over time; they should handle the most difficult behaviors exhibited in the classroom.

In addition to less serious classroom misbehaviors, extreme or dangerous misbehaviors can sometimes occur. A What If? Chart hierarchy must include a preplanned set of consequences (serious behavior clauses) for crisis or out-of-control behaviors, as these misbehaviors can be dangerous as well as greatly disrupt the classroom. Crisis misbehaviors include blatant or defiant noncompliance, a continuing physical fight, carrying a weapon, physical destruction of property (such as fire setting), or long-duration tantrums that include yelling, swearing, or screaming. These behaviors are rare, but their crisis nature requires preplanned consequences that may temporarily remove the student from the classroom.

You may need extra help to implement the serious behavior clause. A two-way school intercom can be used to summon help, or another student can be sent to the principal's office or another teacher's classroom. The steps to request help should be predesigned in a faculty meeting by the faculty and principal before they are implemented.

The What If? Chart also has a place for a Mystery Motivator envelope (see Section 1 of this book) at the bottom as an ultimate reward for the class. The Mystery Motivator can be given randomly once or twice per week to students who have not moved below the first level on the reductive half of the What If? Chart, or it can be given to the student who has improved the most or tried the hardest on an academic assignment that week.

The box to the right of the Mystery Motivator is for teachers to publicly post for themselves the number of positive comments they plan to make to their classes. A minimum of three or four positive comments for every negative comment or consequence is recommended. This means that if frequent negative comments or consequences are necessary, the number of positive comments will need to increase accordingly to maintain this ratio.

Even if negative comments or consequences are infrequent, a minimum of four positive comments per classroom contact hour for each

teacher, aide, or volunteer is suggested. Thus, if teaching is conducted for six hours, 24 positive comments per day by each member of the teaching staff is the minimum (6 hours X 4 comments = 24). This is not 24 positive comments per student, but 24 to the whole class by each staff member.

In the previous example, the number 24 would be written in the box (with a water-based marker if the chart is laminated) to remind and challenge the teaching staff. It's also a good idea for staff members to keep a private tally of their own positive comments, particularly staff who tend to be critical. It is the option of the teaching staff to tell the class what the number means. However, it works well to keep the number a staff secret and to vary the number daily (e.g., 24, 27, 30, 25, etc.).

CLASSROOM BEHAVIOR BINGO

 def•i•ni•tion

Classroom Behavior Bingo (also referred to as Compliance Matrices in *The Tough Kid Book*) is an activity that can be used to dramatically improve selected classroom behaviors for an individual student, for classroom teams, or for the entire class as a whole.

 de•scrip•tion

Classroom Behavior Bingo requires a matrix of numbered squares (e.g., 3 x 3 cells, 4 x 4 cells, or 5 x 5 cells). Copy the Bingo cards provided in this section's reproducible tools (Reproducibles 7-2a–c) for consumable use or laminate them on poster board for reuse.

Steps for Implementing Classroom Behavior Bingo

STEP 1 Define the specific behavior for which Classroom Behavior Bingo is being implemented.

Poor examples include "work hard," "pay attention," and "maintain appropriate behavior in the classroom." Poor examples are vague and/or judgmental.

Better examples include "do what the teacher asks immediately," "turn in completed assignment on time," and "raise your hand and wait for permission to speak." Good examples are descriptive and pinpoint specific behavior.

STEP 2 Select Bingo reinforcers for the day and place them in front of the class near the Bingo card.

TECHNIQUE TIP

Smaller reinforcers, earned more frequently, are more effective initially. ~

STEP 3 Define the Bingo criteria—including the amount or frequency of the behavior required, the amount or quantity of the reinforcer to be provided, and the time limits for earning the Bingo reward.

TECHNIQUE TIP

As in behavioral contracting (see Section 4 of this book), cumulative criteria are usually preferable to consecutive criteria so that students may miss some opportunities of meeting criteria but still have a chance to earn the reward. Cumulative criteria help prevent students from giving up when they make mistakes. ~

STEP 4 Explain the Bingo game to the students who will be participating in the activity. Role-play and demonstrate ways in which the students may meet Bingo criteria and ways in which they may not. Answer any questions the students have regarding the Bingo game.

STEP 5 Each time the students meet Bingo criteria, the individual or group member is permitted to select a number from an opaque container.

TECHNIQUE TIP

Numbers corresponding to numbers on the Bingo card being used may be marked on cardboard tags (e.g., key label tags), on squares of cardboard, on coins, or on poker chips. ~

STEP 6 After a number is drawn, the students then mark the corresponding number on the Bingo card (using a water-based marker if a laminated card is being used). When the numbers selected form any row, column, or diagonal, give the individual or group the specified reinforcers.

STEP 7 When the students become proficient at reaching the criteria, switch the 3 x 3 Bingo card to the 4 x 4 card, and eventually the 5 x 5 card.

Bingo Card Variations

1 The Bingo card system can be used when you desire either a particular criterion to be met several times per day, or several different criteria (e.g., 80% of homework completed and returned in the morning, no reported problems at recess, 80% of in-seat work completed that day, and no more than one name on the board for classroom rule violations).

2 Individual student Bingo cards may be used. With this method, students may meet criteria on individualized target behaviors to earn the right to draw a number.

3 Behavior Bingo cards may be effectively used in combination with Mystery Motivators, Spinners, and grab bags. When the students have completed any row, column, or diagonal, they earn the right to access one of these reinforcement systems (see Sections 1 and 6 of this book and Chapter 2 of *The Tough Kid Book* for additional information).

THE ADVERTISING FOR SUCCESS PROGRAM

 def•i•ni•tion

The Advertising for Success program (also referred to as Public Posting in the first *The Tough Kid Book*) is an intervention that may be used to enhance academic motivation and decrease disruptive behaviors. Advertising for Success primarily involves the display of academic progress scores or behavior measures on a bulletin board or blackboard.

 de•scrip•tion

Academic progress scores can include such items as scores on papers, test scores, points earned for academic work, the number of assignments completed, percentage of assignments completed, and contributions made in class. Behavior measures can include on-task behavior, being on time to class, being prepared to work, the number of warnings received for inappropriate behaviors, appropriate transitions from class to class, and so on.

Steps for Implementing Advertising for Success

STEP 1 Select a visual feedback system to prominently display in the classroom (samples that may be enlarged are provided in this section's reproducible tools, Reproducibles 7-3 through 7-5).

TECHNIQUE TIP

Ideally, the visual feedback chart will be large enough to be seen by students sitting at their desks. The chart should also display a week's worth of data (Monday through Friday) and highlight the week's highest score. The charts provided can be copied for consumable use or laminated on cardboard for reuse from week to week. ~

STEP 2 Decide on a **positive** measure to display. It is important to post only **improvements** in academics or behavior.

TECHNIQUE TIP

Posting positive improvements is much more effective than posting measures that indicate poor performance or inappropriate behavior. A positive measure is also one in which a student is compared against her own past performance and not the performance of other students. If students are routinely compared against each other, the poorer performing students will find the procedure punishing. ~

STEP 3 Decide on a meaningful and precise daily measure.

TECHNIQUE TIP

Measures such as number of problems completed, percentage of improvement, points earned for appropriate behavior, and words read are all good measures. Global measures or information that is dependent on guesswork is poor information to publicly post. ~

STEP 4 Give immediate feedback!

TECHNIQUE TIP

The longer you wait to give feedback to a student, the less effective the Advertising for Success system will be. Feedback should be given as soon as possible. ~

Give positive differential feedback rather than feedback for an absolute level or near-perfect goal. With positive differential feedback, students post improvements against their own best scores and not predetermined criteria.

STEP 5 Develop a system to effectively score students' work so that it can be posted immediately. Peer grading or self-grading may be used to accomplish this requirement.

STEP 6 Verbally praise improvements on the Advertising for Success chart. This is what makes the information meaningful and reinforcing to students.

TECHNIQUE TIP

Use descriptive praise statements such as "Isaac, what a performance! You beat your best weekly score again!" or "Jessica is getting better and better—she did five more problems today!" Poor praise statements are global statements such as "Good job" and "Nice improvement." It is also important to praise students who are having difficulty, but who are improving. ~

TECHNIQUE TIP

Group praise is effective if it is used descriptively and does not single out students who are having difficulty. ~

STEP 7  Encourage peer comments and interaction about publicly posted information. If the students compete against themselves and not each other, spontaneous student comments will be positive.

Advertising for Success Variations

1 Add a tangible reinforcer for students who have improved their scores. Mystery Motivators, Spinners, or grab bags can be used randomly to reinforce students (see Sections 1 and 6 of this book and Chapter 2 of *The Tough Kid Book* for additional information). For example, a student can be selected at random from students who have posted improvements for a particular day. The randomly selected student then receives the daily reinforcer.

2 Some teachers have difficulty grading papers and posting all the students' work each day. To solve this problem, post a chart with several spaces for students' names and randomly select that number of students at the end of the day to have their work graded and the information posted, if improvement was made. With this technique, students are never sure who will have their work posted, so all students work hard each day.

3 Classrooms can be divided into teams and average team results can be posted. For example, three students sitting at a table for math can be designated as a team. At the end of each math period, the students can exchange their papers with each other or another team for grading. The amount of each assignment correctly completed (number of problems) can be averaged and the team's performance can be posted along with their best daily score or best weekly score. A "Team Advertising for Success Chart" (Reproducible 7-4) is provided in this section's reproducible tools for this purpose. A team approach does not require that individual names be posted. However, both team and individual performance can be posted together, if desired.

4 A team-based group contingency can make Advertising for Success even more effective. With a group contingency, the class is divided into teams as previously described; however, a reward or contingency is added for team performance. When group contingencies are used, only team scores should be posted. The teacher must be absolutely sure that all the students on the team can perform the required academic or behavioral task. Group contingencies are best used when students have learned a new skill or behavior and need to practice it. They are less effective when students are still learning how to perform the skill or behavior but have not quite mastered it.

Maximizing the Effectiveness of Advertising for Success

Performance with the Advertising for Success Program can be enhanced by using an Advertising for Success visual display chart that shows several behaviors and/or academic skills for a whole class instead of only one behavior or skill for individual students. For example, the square shown in Figure 7-1 represents four classroom rules pertaining to:

- Correct transition time behavior
- Following teacher directions immediately
- Work completed
- No more than one warning

If the class performs appropriately during an academic period for each of the four specified

"Group contingencies are best used when students have learned a new skill or behavior and need to practice it."

behaviors, a plus (+) is placed in each area. If misbehavior occurs, a minus (-) is placed in that particular area. The advantage of this system is the simplicity of posting for the whole class across several behaviors.

The publicly posted behaviors in this example represent standard classroom rules. You can also combine the Advertising for Success program with an incentive system. You may choose to use the system to improve any behaviors of your choice.

A "Whole Class Performance Chart" is provided in this section's reproducible tools (Reproducible 7-5). Either copy the page for consumable forms or laminate it onto cardboard for reuse.

Figure 7-1

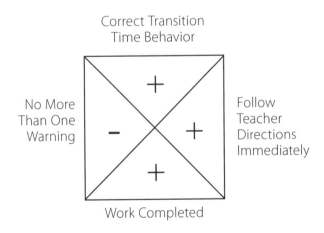

Correct Transition
Time Behavior

No More
Than One
Warning

Follow
Teacher
Directions
Immediately

Work Completed

THE CLASSROOM ACTIVITY SCHEDULE

 def•i•ni•tion

The classroom activity schedule is a specific, planned ordering of learning tasks and other activities during the school day that maximizes students' on-task behavior.

 de•scrip•tion

To have the students remain on task—that is, to be engaged in academic or other activities that demand students' time and attention—will eliminate many behavior problems.

The time not scheduled in a classroom is an open invitation to disruptive behavior. Scheduled academic learning time is critical to the academic success and appropriate classroom behavior of Tough Kids. It is one of the basic proactive variables under teacher control.

Steps for Implementing the Classroom Activity Schedule

STEP 1 Determine the times for *set* activities during the school day over which you do not have control. This may include such activities as lunch, recesses, and planning periods.

STEP 2 Determine *organizational* activities. Organizational activities account for additional noninstructional time. Organizational activities include taking roll, collecting lunch money, sharpening pencils, announcements, flag salute, special permission slips, getting drinks, and going to the restroom. These activities must be planned for and taken care of before instruction takes place, or they will interrupt instruction.

STEP 3 Determine the specific instructional tasks and activities that must take place during the day to meet individual student and district requirements. Estimate the time required to carry out each task.

STEP 4 On paper, organize all tasks/activities identified in Steps 1–3 into a timeframe. A "Classroom Activity Schedule" form (Reproducible 7-6) for this purpose is provided in this section's reproducible tools.

Upon review, your classroom activity schedule should result in a minimum of 70% of the school day being spent on instructional tasks. You may need to adjust the durations and/or number of scheduled activities to meet this recommended figure.

 TECHNIQUE TIP

Many teachers feel overwhelmed at the thought of having students successfully academically engaged for 70% of the day. However, strategies such as classwide peer tutoring (to follow) and cooperative learning make this a realistic goal. ~

 TECHNIQUE TIP

You may prefer to schedule less enjoyable tasks first, after an initial warmup activity (e.g., a simple direction-following task, such as "Simon Says"), or to alternate less enjoyable tasks with more enjoyable ones. You will need to determine which tasks are "enjoyable" and which are less so, since different students will have different preferences. ~

STEP 5 Identify activities which cause changes in the daily classroom activity schedule for individual students and the class as a whole. This may include such activities as speech therapy, physical therapy, mainstream time, schoolwide events, and vacation days.

STEP 6 Post the schedule of daily activities/class periods in a conspicuous place in the room. Make certain the print is large enough to be seen from any part of the room.

 TECHNIQUE TIP

For secondary students, provide an 8.5" X 11" copy of the classroom activity schedule for their notebooks. Post an alternate schedule next to the main schedule for the changeable aspects of the school day identified in Step 5. ~

STEP 7 Make certain that the students understand the classroom activity schedule. Telling them is not enough. Review the schedule several times before assuming they know the routine. Initially, this may require a daily review. Question them about the schedule, role-play examples and non-examples of expectations regarding the schedule, and give students opportunities to ask questions.

STEP 8 Once the classroom activity schedule has been explained and posted, stick with it! Time for a particular activity may vary, but stay with the routine schedule.

STEP 9 A great deal of time can be wasted if the transition between different activities is not managed efficiently and smoothly.

 TECHNIQUE TIP

Minimize transition time by: (1) having materials organized and ready, (2) confidently stopping one activity and initiating the next, (3) increasing monitoring of students during transition times (praising and recognizing those who transition quickly—e.g., "Danny and Brenda got their books, went to the group, and are waiting quietly for me. Way to go!"), and (4) planning activities at which students can succeed so that they will be enthusiastic about beginning the next activity. ~

STEP 10 After the classroom activity schedule has been established, do not hesitate to make changes if it is not working satisfactorily. When making changes, post copies of the revised schedule (and give secondary students their own revised copy). Make certain that the students understand the new routine (following those procedures detailed in Step 7).

Maximizing the Effectiveness of the Classroom Activity Schedule

1 Because students may become restless, sleepy, bored, or inattentive during prolonged periods of inactivity, consider the planned level of physical activity during the day, particularly with younger students. Plan for some physical activity every hour or so, even if it is only to stand and stretch or get a drink. Be certain that students also have time during their day for physical games and more strenuous activity.

2 In an attempt to keep student interest high, do not build so much variety into the classroom activity schedule that the students are constantly guessing about what is going to happen next. Too much variety may decrease on-task behavior and increase transition time. Too little variety, on the other hand, will make the classroom a boring or unpleasant place to be.

CLASSWIDE PEER TUTORING
def•i•ni•tion

Classwide peer tutoring is a one-to-one teaching arrangement in which peers serve as instructional agents for classmates or other students in an academic setting. Peer tutoring instruction can be used effectively for either academic or social skills.

de•scrip•tion

Peer tutoring can provide a means for structured practice or review, for students to serve as monitors for other students, and to reinforce teacher-directed instruction. It has been effectively used in both regular and special education settings.

Steps for Implementing Classwide Peer Tutoring

STEP 1 Divide the class into two or more teams. The teams may be designated by a name, a number, or a color.

STEP 2 Pair each team member with a peer "partner" from his or her team. Select and reassign peer pairs once each week.

TECHNIQUE TIP

Be careful to pair Tough Kids with students who consistently display appropriate behavior and not with other Tough Kids! ~

STEP 3 First decide on a subject for tutoring, and then select a 30-minute period of the day for the program. (Within the 30 minutes allotted, the peer will tutor the partner for ten minutes and the partner will tutor the peer for ten minutes. And ten minutes will be spent by both the peer and tutor counting points and posting results.)

STEP 4 Train the assigned student pairs to conduct the tutoring sessions. First, demonstrate the correct tutoring process for the students:

a. Have student pairs sit next to or across from each other during tutoring sessions.
b. Teach the tutors to praise when their partner responds correctly.
c. Teach the tutors a correction procedure for errors (e.g., give the correct answer, lead the partner through the correct answer, have the partner give the correct answer independently, praise the partner for a correct response, and move on).
d. Teach the tutors to use a score sheet (see Reproducible 7-7 in this section's reproducible tools) to keep track of correct responses.
e. Teach the tutors to award points for correct responses.

STEP 5 Carry out the daily 30-minute peer tutoring sessions. Tell each pair who will tutor first. The tutor will monitor the partner's performance (e.g., listen to oral reading, correct errors, and award points for correct performance). Signal at the end of ten minutes that the partner is to now monitor the peer's performance.

TECHNIQUE TIP

Circulate among the pairs of students during peer tutoring sessions and award them bonus points for correctly following the tutoring procedures and appropriate behavior. ~

STEP 6 When both ten-minute tutoring sessions are over, have each member of the pairs count her own and her partner's points. Have each pair of students add their scores together for a daily total (see Figure 7-2). When you call on the pair, have them verbally report their points earned, including any bonus points.

STEP 7 Publicly post tutoring pair and team scores (see the Advertising for Success charts in this section's reproducible tools). Praise and encourage improvement.

STEP 8 Announce a winning team every day and every week. Weekly team scores are determined by adding daily team scores. Daily and weekly rewards for winning teams may be given in the form of privileges (e.g., to be excused two minutes early for recess), small edible treats, Mystery Motivators, Spinners, or Chart Moves (see Sections 1 and 6 of this book).

STEP 9 At the end of the first few sessions, demonstrate for the students any procedures requiring clarification. Discuss how the tutoring sessions went, and answer any questions that the students may have.

STEP 10 Assess individual student performance on instructional material presented in tutoring sessions regularly. Regular quizzes on tutoring material will keep you informed of individual student progress.

Troubleshooting Classwide Peer Tutoring

Observe the tutoring pairs closely for those students who are not making adequate progress on the tutored material. If you observe problems, make one or more of the following adjustments: (1) make certain that the tutoring procedures are being carried out correctly, (2) consider changing the reinforcers, or (3) provide additional practice on the material with increased tutoring time or through other teacher-directed activities.

Making Classwide Peer Tutoring Even Better

Give the student pairs several practice opportunities under close supervision before expecting them to function independently. Give specific praise and feedback to the student pairs.

Figure 7-2

Student: Rocky Rhode   Week of: Oct. 16

Partner: Billy Budd   Team: Buzzards

	Points	+ Bonus Points	= Daily Total Points	+ Partner's Total Points	= Posting Score
M	卌 卌 ||| 13	卌 5	18	16	34
T	卌 卌 卌 |||| 19	||| 3	22	17	39
W					
TH					
F					

BEHAVIORAL OBSERVATION

 def•i•ni•tion

Behavioral observation is the collecting of a sample of problem behavior in the setting in which it occurs. No recall from memory or judgment as to its severity is required with behavioral observations. As the behavior occurs, it is simply recorded.

 de•scrip•tion

Behavioral observation of a student is possibly one of the most accurate and valid of all

"If the behavior occurs, it is simply recorded."

available assessment measures. One simple behavioral observation approach that allows normative comparisons is the response discrepancy observation method. This system allows a behavior discrepancy (difference) comparison between a target student (suspected Tough Kid) and his classroom peers. An observation form (Reproducible 7-8) to conduct this type of observation is included in this section's reproducible tools.

The observation form is based on observing the on- and off-task behavior of a target student. The observer should be familiar with the on-task and off-task behavior codes listed on the bottom of the form. The basic class activity for the particular observation should be filled in.

The actual observations are based on ten-second intervals (each box in the center of the form represents ten seconds), with 90 of these intervals included in the 15-minute observation period on which this form is based. The top interval box is for the referred target student, and the bottom interval box is for a randomly selected same-sex peer.

For each ten-second interval, the target student is observed along with the peer. If the target student is on task for the entire ten-second interval,

then an on-task code (i.e., a dot) is recorded. However, if the target student is off-task during the ten-second interval, the appropriate off-task code is recorded in the interval. Only one off-task behavior is recorded for each ten-second interval. If more off-task behaviors occur, they are ignored until the next ten-second interval. The same recording process occurs for the same-sex peer during the same ten-second interval for each box.

At the end of a 15-minute observation sample, a record of total on- and off-task behaviors is collected for the target student. The actual on-task percentage can be easily calculated for the 15-minute observation sample with the following formula: divide the number of on-task intervals by the total number of on- and off-task intervals and multiply by one hundred. This equals the actual on-task percentage.

Formula:

$$\left(\frac{\text{\# of on-task intervals}}{\text{\# of on- and off-task intervals}} \right) \times 100 = \% \text{ on task}$$

In addition, a micro-norm or sample for on- and off-task behavior has been simultaneously collected on the same-sex peers in the classroom and can be similarly calculated. This allows a comparison between a suspected Tough Kid and his or her peers. If the student is on-task 60% or less of the time and his peer's average is 85% or more, you know you have a distractible student.

However, if both the suspected Tough Kid's and the peer's averages for on-task behavior are below 60%, the problem may be a more general classroom management problem.

General Interventions Reproducible Tools

Both Spanish and English versions of all REPRODUCIBLE TOOLS appear on the CD.

What If? Chart

WHAT IF YOU DO?	WHAT IF YOU DON'T?
_____	_____
_____	_____
_____	_____
_____	_____
_____	_____
_____	_____
_____	_____
_____	_____

?

MYSTERY
MOTIVATOR

Serious Behavior Clause(s):

_____

_____

_____

See pp. 111 and 112 for suggestions for use.

Classroom Behavior Bingo Card

1	2	3
4	5	6
7	8	9

Classroom Behavior Bingo Card

1	2	3	4
5	6	7	8
9	10	11	12
13	14	15	16

See pp. 112–114 for suggestions for use.

Tough Kid Tool Box

K-6

FOR GRADES

Classroom Behavior Bingo Card

1	2	3	4	5
6	7	8	9	10
11	12	13	14	15
16	17	18	19	20
21	22	23	24	25

See pp. 112–114 for suggestions for use.

Advertising for Success Chart

Student Name(s)	Monday	Tuesday	Wednesday	Thursday	Friday	BEST SCORE

Tough Kid Tool Box

FOR GRADES
K-6

Team Advertising for Success Chart

	Monday	Tuesday	Wednesday	Thursday	Friday	BEST SCORE
Team 1						
Team 2						
Team 3						
Team 4						
Team 5						

See pp. 114–117 for suggestions for use.

Tough Kid Tool Box

K-6

FOR GRADES

Advertising for Success Whole Class Performance Chart

Date _____   Class Period or Subject _____

Classroom Activity Schedule

TIME	DAYS	ACTIVITIES	ASSIGNMENTS
SPECIAL ACTIVITY			

See pp. 117–119 for suggestions for use.

Tough Kid Tool Box

4 - 6

FOR GRADES

Classwide Peer Tutoring Score Sheets

Student _____ Week of _____

Partner _____ Team _____

	Points	+ Bonus Points	= Daily Total Points	+ Partner's Total Points	= Posting Score
M					
T					
W					
TH					
F					

Student _____ Week of _____

Partner _____ Team _____

	Points	+ Bonus Points	= Daily Total Points	+ Partner's Total Points	= Posting Score
M					
T					
W					
TH					
F					

See pp. 119–121 for suggestions for use.

Tough Kid Tool Box

Behavior Observation Form

Target Student _____ M/F _____ Grade _____

School _____ Teacher _____ Date _____

Observer _____ Position _____

Class Activity _____

❏ Teacher-directed whole class   ❏ Teacher-directed small class   ❏ Independent work session

DIRECTIONS: Each box represents a ten-second interval. Observe each student **once**, then record the data. This is a partial interval recording. If possible, collect data for the full 15 minutes under a teacher-directed or independent condition. If this is not possible, put a slash when the classroom condition changes. **Classmates observed must be the same sex as the target student.**

					1					2					3
Target Student															
Peer*															

					4					5					6
Target Student															
Peer*															

					7					8					9
Target Student															
Peer*															

					10					11					12
Target Student															
Peer*															

					13					14					15
Target Student															
Peer*															

*Randomly selected classmate of the same sex

NOTE: To observe class, begin with the first same-sex student in row 1. Record each subsequent same-sex student in following intervals. Data reflect an average of classroom behavior. **Skip unobservable students.**

ON-TASK CODES: • = Eye contact with teacher or task and performing the requested task.

OFF-TASK CODES:

    T = **Talking Out/Noise:** Inappropriate verbalization or making sounds with object, mouth, or body.

    O = **Out of Seat:** Student fully or partially out of assigned seat without teacher permission.

    I = **Inactive:** Student not engaged with assigned task and passively waiting, sitting, etc.

    N = **Noncompliance:** Breaking a classroom rule or not following teacher directions within 15 seconds.

    P = **Playing With Object:** Manipulating objects without teacher permission.

    + = **Positive Teacher Interaction:** One-on-one positive comment, smiling, touching, or gesture.

    - = **Negative Teacher Interaction:** One-on-one reprimand, implementing negative consequence, or negative gesture.

    / = **Neutral Teacher Interaction:** One-on-one expressionless teacher interaction, no approval or disapproval expressed, directions given.

See pp. 121 and 122 for suggestions for use.

Tough Kid Series

Tough Kids challenge your rules, your authority, and your patience. If you're in need of strategies and techniques to address student aggression, noncompliance, lack of motivation, poor academic performance, and other tough problems, look no further. The Tough Kid Series provides practical, classroom-tested, easy-to-implement strategies for managing and motivating those tough students so your class can focus on learning.

Call 1-866-542-1490

Shop online at www.pacificnwpublish.com

The Tough Kid Book: Practical Classroom Management Strategies (2nd edition)

Ginger Rhode, Ph.D., William R. Jenson, Ph.D., and H. Kenton Reavis, Ed.D.

The original Tough Kid book is newly revised and updated with more creative techniques that you can use immediately to deal with tough classroom behaviors such as aggression, noncompliance, tantrums, and more. The book covers both positive procedures that reward desired student behavior as well as reductive techniques that stop problem behaviors.

The Tough Kid New Teacher Book

Ginger Rhode, Ph.D., William R. Jenson, Ph.D., and Daniel P. Morgan, Ph.D.

Get your first year of teaching off to a great start with this easy-to-read guide to the essentials of classroom behavior management. Learn simple yet effective tactics to make any class pay attention, respect you and each other, and follow your classroom rules.

The Tough Kid Bully Blockers Book: 15-Minute Lessons for Preventing and Reducing Bullying

Julie Bowen, Ph.D., Paula Ashcraft, Ph.D., William R. Jenson, Ph.D., and Ginger Rhode, Ph.D.

FOR GRADES **1 – 6**

Tough Kids can be bullies, and they can also be victims of bullying. This positive and proactive program guides you through implementing a bully-blocking program in your school or classroom. A field-tested set of 15-minute lessons equip students—whether bullies, victims, or bystanders—with six skills to reverse bullying behavior. A companion CD includes reproducible posters, forms, homework assignments, and worksheets.

Bully Blocker Shorts

This set of quick-draw videos demonstrates the six skills for preventing and reducing bullying presented in *The Tough Kid Bully Blocker Book*. *The Bully Blocker Shorts* stand alone, but are a perfect resource for previewing and reviewing skills taught in *The Tough Kid Bully Blocker Book*. You and your students will want to watch the Shorts over and over.

The Tough Kid Social Skills Book

Susan M. Sheridan, Ph.D.

FOR GRADES **3 – 8**

When students don't know how to resolve conflict, express frustration, or interact with others, they have difficulty with schoolwork and in their personal lives. This Tough Kid volume addresses ten specific social skills, including dealing with teasing, using self-control, solving arguments, and joining in. Improve the quality of your classroom and a student's chance to succeed in life. *The Tough Kid Social Skills Book* is a great place to start! Includes a CD of reproducible forms.

Additional Resources

The Tough Kid Parent Book

William R. Jenson, Ph.D., Ginger Rhode, Ph.D., and
Melanie Hepworth Neville, M.A.

Any kid can be a Tough Kid—arguing, throwing tantrums, ignoring what you ask, frequently getting in trouble. This book guides parents through a step-by-step process for managing challenging behavior. Use these positive techniques to eliminate arguing and noncompliance as well as address more serious behaviors such as stealing, fire setting, bed wetting, smoking, drinking, and drug use.

Social Skills for the Tough Kid: Tips and Tools for Parents

Susan M. Sheridan, Ph.D.

This book was compiled over several years as a direct result of the author's work with parents of children who had difficulties making and keeping friends. It contains tried-and-true strategies to help parents teach their children important social skills. These strategies are invaluable in helping parents develop a framework for talking to their children about friendship problems and for encouraging their children to use social skills in everyday situations. These efforts improve not only the children's social behavior but also the relationship between parent and child.

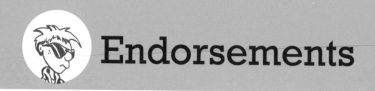

Endorsements

What educators have to say about The Tough Kid Tool Box . . .

"*The Tough Kid Tool Box* is an invaluable resource for everyone working with children and youth with challenging behaviors. Student services personnel—resource teachers, counselors, behavior specialists, and school psychologists in particular—as well as classroom teachers will find the Tool Box a useful resource document in the development and implementation of appropriate program plans. *The Tough Kid Tool Box* is clearly formatted and 'jam-packed' with positive, practical techniques and strategies that are motivational and fun! These well-defined strategies can be readily incorporated into IEPs and behavioral plans, and customized to support individual student outcomes and interventions for the entire class. One of the most valuable features of the *The Tough Kid Tool Box* is the number of reproducible forms to be used for data collection and data tracking purposes. Forms for student self-monitoring and a wide range of behavioral contract forms also are included. An accompanying CD contains electronic versions of each form that can be completed as appropriate directly on the computer. The authors are to be applauded for their timely revision of this comprehensive and highly recommended resource!"

Candace Borger
Administrator, Educational Support Services, St. James-Assiniboia School Division, Winnipeg, Manitoba, Canada

"There is nothing more difficult for a teacher and classroom than a disruptive student. Student behaviors can appear to be a mysterious set of unchangeable circumstances that create chaos and disruption. Schools are directed to use evidence-based interventions that frequently are not practical in a school setting. Enter the Tough Kid Series. Dr. Jenson, Dr. Rhode, and Dr. Reavis have created magic by setting in motion evidence-based practices in a fun, engaging method that is simple to implement and practical for classroom management. Kids, even 'Tough Kids,' love them. Teachers are empowered to create a positive learning environment with the most challenging students. I don't know how any classroom today can function without the knowledge and power that comes from these pages."

Dr. Sally LaRue
Director of Educational Support Services, Humble Independent School District, Humble, Texas

"*The Tough Kid Tool Box* is a superb behavior management resource for educators. The strategies are sound and based on solid scientific principles; the activities and tactics are positive, fun, and effective. Teachers will find *The Tough Kid Tool Box* to be an invaluable addition to their professional library, something they will turn to frequently to help them deal effectively with their challenging students and to create a fun, safe, and positive learning environment in their classroom. I recommend this program highly."

Ken Merrell, Ph.D.
Professor and Co-Director, School Psychology Program, and Head, Department of Special Education and Clinical Sciences, University of Oregon